OXFORD
INDIA SHORT
INTRODUCTIONS
KASHMIR

The Oxford India Short
Introductions are concise,
stimulating, and accessible guides
to different aspects of India.
Combining authoritative analysis,
new ideas, and diverse perspectives,
they discuss subjects which are
topical yet enduring, as also
emerging areas of study and debate.

OTHER TITLES IN THE SERIES

Employment in India
Ajit K. Ghose

Indian Federalism
Loiuse Tillin

Surrogacy
Anindita Majumdar

Jawaharlal Nehru
Rudrangshu Mukherjee

The Partition of India
Haimanti Roy

Indian Nuclear Policy
Harsh V. Pant and Yogesh Joshi

Indian Democracy
Suhas Palshikar

Indian National Security
Chris Ogden

Bollywood
M.K. Raghavendra

The Indian Middle Class
Surinder S. Jodhka and Aseem Prakash

Indian Foreign Policy
Sumit Ganguly

For more information, visit our website:
https://india.oup.com/content/series/o/
oxford-india-short-introductions/

OXFORD
INDIA SHORT
INTRODUCTIONS

KASHMIR

CHITRALEKHA ZUTSHI

OXFORD
UNIVERSITY PRESS

OXFORD
UNIVERSITY PRESS

Oxford University Press is a department of the University of Oxford.
It furthers the University's objective of excellence in research, scholarship,
and education by publishing worldwide. Oxford is a registered trademark of
Oxford University Press in the UK and in certain other countries.

Published in India by
Oxford University Press
22 Workspace, 2nd Floor, 1/22 Asaf Ali Road, New Delhi 110002, India

© Oxford University Press 2019

The moral rights of the author have been asserted.

First Edition published in 2019

ISBN-13 (print edition): 978-0-19-012141-9
ISBN-10 (print edition): 0-19-012141-6

ISBN-13 (eBook): 978-0-19-099046-6
ISBN-10 (eBook): 0-19-099046-5

Typeset in 11/14.3 Bembo Std
by Tranistics Data Technologies, Kolkata 700 091
Printed in India by Replika Press Pvt. Ltd

Contents

Contents

Introduction

The Idea of Kashmir

Kashmir holds a special place in our imaginations, whether as a paradise on earth or a deadly conflict zone, or a range of ideas in between. This book seeks to understand why and how we came to attribute these characteristics to Kashmir, and through that, to understand Kashmir itself in its multiple definitions. This endeavour has to begin with the question of what/where is Kashmir? The answer depends on the historical moment, since the geographical extent of what we call Kashmir has shifted through the centuries depending on political circumstances and the political entities that consolidated their rule over this region that lies at the crossroads between Central and South Asia. However, whether an independent kingdom, a province of the Mughal or Afghan Empires, a princely state in British India, or a state in India, the Kashmir Valley has remained at the heart of all these entities that have been referred to as Kashmir.

The Kashmir Valley, formed by the River Jhelum and its tributaries, measures a mere 89 by 25 miles, but has exercised tremendous influence over the history of the region due to its geographical location nestled within the Himalayan ranges, which form a natural protective barrier around it. Srinagar, located in the Valley, has thus served as the capital of multiple imperial and other political entities that have existed in the wider region. As a result, the Valley has been the centre of vibrant political, religious, and cultural exchanges, which have produced a continuous multilingual literary and historical tradition; this in turn has played a significant role in defining Kashmir, with the Valley itself, not surprisingly, serving as its central axis. As we shall see in the book, the Valley has been instrumental in the way that we define and understand Kashmir, which is also why Kashmir and the Kashmir Valley are terms that are often used interchangeably.

Kashmir, thus, is as much an idea as it is a geographical place, and this short book traces the shifting contours of both through history. It highlights not just how Kashmir was defined in particular periods, but also why and by whom. In the process, it brings to light the ever-changing and yet interconnected political and religious institutions and ideologies, literary traditions, and social classes that shaped the history of this region. It argues that Kashmir as we know and understand it today is a composite of multiple ideas and variable boundaries that were produced in specific historical and political contexts, the shape and direction of which, in turn, those very ideas influenced. Thus, what it means to be a Kashmiri, too, changed over the course of time, with individuals and groups asserting their belonging to Kashmir—a variously imagined entity— and the concomitant identity, for a variety of reasons. At all times, the idea of Kashmir developed through a synergistic conversation between these insiders and those deemed outsiders, who have thus contributed in equally significant ways to how Kashmir has been defined and understood.

In uncovering the discursive strategies through which Kashmir has been defined, the book challenges the received wisdom that it is a fixed entity that has displayed unique physical, political, and religious characteristics throughout its past. Instead, it demonstrates that Kashmir's uniqueness was (and remains) central to its very definition because this idea has served, and continues to serve, significant political purposes. The assertion of Kashmir's peerless physical beauty due to its geographic location and its distinct religious culture, among other features, has allowed individuals and institutions to claim for it a centrality in South and Central Asia and within much larger empires, which it would have otherwise lacked due to its size and location. Furthermore, Kashmir's association with a special status has intensified in the recent past in the context of the conflict between India and Pakistan over the region since 1947, with each state placing it at the heart of its nationalist aspirations.

This book demonstrates that Kashmir is a place like any other, with a distinct but not unique past. Most importantly, in its indigenous intellectual tradition, it appears as the centre of literary and political culture, and not a distant frontier to be policed and secured. It became the focus of a conflict not because it is special or because it is an unruly borderland, but rather because of political developments in the last decade of British colonial rule and the moment of decolonization of the Indian subcontinent. The parties involved in the conflict, however, have laid claim to and refashioned the narrative of uniqueness that defined Kashmir and served particular political needs in the past, to justify their own claims to it in the present.

The book unfolds roughly chronologically following the multiple ideas associated with Kashmir and its changing geographical boundaries through the centuries. It begins by charting the emergence of the idea of Kashmir as a sacred space in its Sanskrit and

Persian narrative traditions from the seventh up to the sixteenth centuries, and the institutional locations and political imperatives that gave sustenance to this idea. This particularly potent idea gave the rulers of Kashmir, a small kingdom in the northern reaches of the subcontinent, the ability to claim it as an ideal Brahmanical space, or an ideal Islamic space, thereby endowing the land with a centrality it would otherwise not possess.

As the rest of the book establishes, the idea of Kashmir as a privileged locale with a distinctive landscape has perhaps been the most enduring one associated with it, invoked in its narrative tradition and political culture and incorporated into subsequent definitions of the place to serve a variety of political objectives. The next chapter turns to the definition of Kashmir as *mulk*, or homeland, through the long eighteenth century, as the decline of the Mughal Empire and Kashmir's incorporation into the Afghan Empire, followed by the Sikh Kingdom, brought about significant changes to its political and economic landscapes. 'Kashmir' and 'Kashmiri' emerged as distinct historical categories at this moment, which while unfree, could exist outside the realm of larger regional spaces or imperial entities.

This distinctiveness remained in place even after Kashmir became part of a new imperial entity, the princely state of Jammu and Kashmir, in the mid-nineteenth century. Chapter 3 details the fashioning of this new political entity by its Dogra rulers and Kashmir's place within it. Even as the Dogras claimed the Kashmir Valley as the heart of their newly acquired kingdom, with Srinagar as its summer capital, they made no attempt to include Kashmir or Kashmiris, particularly Kashmiri Muslims, into their ideology of legitimacy or their institutions of government. Religious—not as much regional—identity thus became the focus, as Kashmiri Muslims in particular debated the contours of their community and the definition of Islam as practised in Kashmir.

As Chapter 4 illustrates, however, the idea of Kashmir (defined as the Valley) as an exceptional region was cemented in the long nineteenth century in the global imperial arena, largely through the efforts of outsiders, such as orientalist scholars, European travellers, and merchants. Through their study of Kashmir's Sanskrit texts, admiration of its geographical features, and the marketing and consumption of its fine manufactures, these individuals spread Kashmir's fame as a unique region in the subcontinent. By the early twentieth century, the idea of Kashmir as a tourist destination par excellence—a pure, untrammelled paradise to be enjoyed and explored by people from around the world—was firmly in place.

In reality, this was a moment of great economic upheaval and political tumult for the people of the princely state of Jammu and Kashmir. Chapter 5 details the emergence of the political movement against the Dogra regime in the late 1920s that demanded economic uplift and eventually political freedom for Kashmir, now defined as *watan*, or nation. Initially appealing to Muslims across the princely state, by the late 1930s, the movement broadened to include all Kashmiris—regardless of religion and class—striving for a redressal of their economic and political grievances. The leadership of the Kashmir Valley, Jammu, and other regions jostled to gain control over the movement's direction in an attempt to represent their own constituents' distinct demands. This raised the question of whether the Kashmiri nation could be defined more expansively to include regions besides the Kashmir Valley and communities other than upper-class Muslims. As British Indian organizations entered the fray, the movement splintered along regional, religious, and class lines, eventually leading it to founder on these very divisions by the time Independence, Partition, and along with it, the end of British paramountcy over princely states rolled around. By 1949, Jammu and Kashmir was a fragmented entity.

It is the resultant fragments that form the topic of the next chapter, which examines the post-1949 period from the perspective of the tenuous associations of these political entities with India and Pakistan. The relationships between India and its state of Jammu and Kashmir, and between Pakistan and Azad Kashmir and Gilgit-Baltistan—neither provinces nor fully autonomous entities within its jurisdiction—are determined by the terms of the dispute, according to which both India and Pakistan claim sole sovereignty over the entire territory of the erstwhile princely state. This has led India to forcefully integrate Jammu and Kashmir into the union at the expense of the democratic rights of the state's inhabitants while Pakistan has been reluctant to integrate Azad Kashmir and Gilgit–Baltistan, thereby rendering them into indeterminate entities whose inhabitants have little political power. The chapter thus reveals the diversity and complexities of the relationships that comprise the Kashmir 'dispute', which it argues is far more than simply a bilateral dispute between India and Pakistan.

The final chapter takes a closer look at contemporary politics in the Indian state of Jammu and Kashmir, in particular from the perspective of the resistance movement to the Indian state in the Kashmir Valley that gathered force in the late 1980s. As earlier chapters illustrate, the conditions for this revolt were laid down much before the 1980s, leading to myriad forms of resistance to the Indian state in the 1960s and 1970s.

By the late 1980s, the resistance had taken on a renewed ferocity, and the chapter charts its multiple phases as Kashmir became ever more closely aligned with the Kashmir Valley and its demand for *azaadi* (independence), itself variously defined, from Indian postcolonial colonial rule. Beginning as a popular, violent upsurge against the corrupt, inept, and puppet regimes that ran the state and denied Kashmiris their basic political rights since 1947, the insurgency has now transformed into everyday resistance in the streets against India and its heavy-handed military response.

The last two chapters of the book capture the tremendous cost of the dispute over Jammu and Kashmir for the people of this region, who have paid dearly for it, with their lives, the lives of their loved ones, their property, their rights, and most of all, their tranquillity. Most of them have been drawn unwillingly into this tussle over 'Kashmir', whether they identify their land as Kashmir and themselves as Kashmiris, as in the case of the Kashmir Valley, or they do not, as in the case of Gilgit-Baltistan, Jammu, and Ladakh. However, they have not taken this in silence, as they have led and continue to lead movements of protest and resistance against the regimes that control their lives. This reminds us that in the contemporary moment, Kashmir is not just a territory or a conflict; it is as much a group of people who have been forced into becoming agents of their own oppression due to the lack of resolution of this dispute.

By tracing the idea of Kashmir in its varied iterations—a sacred space, a homeland, a princely state, an exceptional region, a nation, and a divided entity that comprises a dispute and a people—this short work illustrates that Kashmir has been a product, at different historical moments, of dialogue and dissension among diverse ideologies, institutions, languages, and political entities. It cautions us, most importantly, to not read the current dispute into its history and thus render its past into a civilizational struggle between Hinduism and Islam. Doing so does great violence to the rich interconnectedness that, as this book reveals, has characterized the past of this place, which successive groups of people have called home.

1

Kashmir as Sacred Space

The holy region of Kasmira is possessed of all the
sacred places. There are sacred lakes of the Nagas and
the holy mountains; there are holy rivers and also
the holy lakes; there are highly sacred temples and
also the hermitages attached to them. In the centre
flows, making as it were the parting of the hair,
the Vitasta—the highest goddess visibly born of
the Himalaya.

—*Nilamata Purana*[1]

The idea of Kashmir as an especially blessed sacred
space, as described in the preceding quote from
Nilamata Purana, has been cemented in Kashmir's
interconnected narrative tradition through the
centuries in multiple languages. This idea is not merely
a literary or religio-cultural idea, although it is very
much a part of Kashmiris' own self-understanding of

their land, but a deeply spatial and political idea that has been deployed by a variety of actors in the service of state and institutional imperatives. These individuals and groups have utilized the idea as a means to redefine the boundaries of Kashmir, to claim a special status for it in the larger community of kingdoms in the northern Indian subcontinent and Central Asia, and to re-situate the Kashmir polity at the centre of the subcontinental and Islamic worlds. This chapter charts the making of Kashmir as sacred space as an element of larger and intensely interconnected literary and political processes, whereby narratives and imperial entities mutually created and legitimized each other.

Aryavarta

Kashmir's prolific Sanskrit tradition played a significant role in defining the polity of Kashmir by designating it as a specific kind of sacred space. Several scholars have written about the centrality of *Nilamata Purana*— one or more interconnected narratives most likely composed in the sixth or seventh century—to the process of the transformation of Kashmir from a barbaric outpost on the margins of northern India to an auspicious imperial entity that claimed to be the centre of India, or Aryavarta itself (Ghai 1968; Inden 2000; Sharma 2008). The political changes in the

2

northern subcontinent and Kashmir at the time were not simply reflected in this narrative but were utilized to claim a pivotal and special place for Kashmir, which it had not previously occupied in the Indian imperial and cosmographic universes.

The king of Kashmir in whose court *Nilamata Purana* was composed was most likely Durlabhavana (c. 626/7–662/3), who was not only from a new dynasty, but also ascended to the throne at a time—with the Gupta polity and the Hunas in decline—when Kashmir was poised to register itself as an independent kingdom in northern India. Durlabhavana used this moment to gain control over a variety of adjacent territories, and through *Nilamata Purana*, situated Kashmir, in Ronald Inden's words, as 'the center of an imperial Theist kingdom consisting of the countries of the northern quarter of India' (2000: 77). The narrative was a critical means through which Durlabhavana established his own kingship within Kashmir while also repositioning Kashmir within an Indian imperial space.

This was accomplished in *Nilamata Purana* by outlining specific rituals to be performed by the king that would initiate him into kingship, and by endowing Kashmir with qualities that made it a territory equally, if not more, sacred than the most sacred parts of the subcontinent. As Mahesh Sharma has illustrated so well, the narrative recast the iconography of rivers and the rituals associated with them, particularly at points of confluence and at their banks, to establish 'a sacred space parallel to the sub-continental cosmos' (2008: 126).

The *Nilamata Purana* glorifies Kashmir as the incarnation of Uma herself, exemplified in the River Vitasta (Jhelum), which merges with Hara (Shiva), exemplified in the River Sindh (Indus), thus transforming Kashmir into the holiest of all pilgrimage sites. Not only was Kashmir as a whole a *tirtha* (pilgrimage site or a crossing mediating between heaven and earth), the *Nilamata Purana* gives a detailed list of the tirthas within it, thus marking almost every inch of its territory as sacred. Most significantly, Kashmir's sacredness was not limited to its territory, but transformed it, as Inden notes, into 'the condensed icon and the origin of the Middle Region itself' and thus the primary divine space in the subcontinent (2008: 545).

Taking these ideas further, King Lalitaditya (c. 724/5–760/1) claimed universal kingship, while transforming Kashmir's built landscape to reflect its status as *Aryavarta*. He built his capital Parihaspura at the confluence of the Vitasta and Sindh Rivers, and much as these two rivers had been made synonymous with the Yamuna and Ganga respectively in the *Nilamata Purana*, his capital was meant to represent a new Kanauj. Another text, the *Visnudharmottara Purana*, played a significant role in crystallizing this imperial project by claiming all of the subcontinent as Lalitaditya's, and by extension, Kashmir's, domain, and Kashmir as the new centre of Vaishnavism. This was not just a textual conquest, since Lalitaditya did indeed conquer parts of India, including Kanauj, due to the weakening of the Chalukyas as the paramount power in early eighth-century India (Inden 2000: 82–6).

Not only did textual narratives such as *Nilamata Purana* bolster political claims, but equally significantly, as Sharma reminds us, they were a way for marginal regions such as Kashmir to be claimed as spaces for the assertion of Brahmanism. This explains why purification was the central tenet in these texts, to be achieved by visiting pilgrimage sites usually tied to rivers and other water bodies and performing rituals associated with them. Nevertheless, the *Nilamata Purana* and other Sanskrit narratives reflected and celebrated the plurality of early Kashmir's religious landscape. Although a Shaivite narrative, *Nilamata Purana* attempts to provide equal space to competing sectarian ideologies, especially Vaishnavism, while also accommodating contemporary and previous traditions and practices influenced by Mahayana Buddhism and Tantrism (see Ghai 1968: 23).

Powerful tax-exempt institutions, such as *agraharas*, *mathas*, and monasteries, granted by the rulers to these religious sects, not only legitimized kingship, but also controlled vast tracts of land, and through that the labour of the masses, particularly the immiserated peasantry. Due to its geography, there was little arable land in Kashmir and the peasants toiled away on miniscule plots under a heavy burden of taxation with little recourse. Therefore, many of the rituals outlined in the *Nilamata Purana* were designed to ensure a regular supply of labour, surplus, gifts, and other ritual obligations to the religious institutions and their managers at critical times during the year. This administrative machinery funnelled resources from the people to the state and protected against rebellion (Hangloo 2000: 23). As the tax burden continued to increase, however, and the power of new social classes grew, the religio-political consensus between rulers and Brahmans disintegrated, and Kashmir entered a more chaotic time in its history.

Especially Blessed Landscape/
Peripheral Kingdom

Working in tandem, Kashmir's narrative and political traditions generated and embedded the idea of Kashmir as a privileged locale, every physical spot of which was sacred and where multiple religious traditions flourished together. As a result, long after it had ceased to be a political centre of a subcontinental imperial formation, these ideas continued to hold sway in Kashmir. Written during an especially turbulent time in Kashmir's history, Kalhana's *Rajatarangini* (1148–9) gave fresh voice to these ideas in an attempt to create the image of an ideal Kashmir in the past that was far different from the political dissension and violence that characterized its recent past and present. Situated within a diverse literary milieu that was derived from the practices and narratives generated within a plural Kashmir, the historical poem seamlessly combines the mythical, political, social, spiritual, and geographical to assert a vision of Kashmir's uniqueness in a messy present.

After the death of King Avantivarman (r. 855–83), the old social order came under serious pressure, and Kashmir's central authority began to decline as a result of the revolts by Damaras (landed chieftans), Tantrins (hill Rajputs employed in the armies of Kashmiri kings), and other groups. Damaras and Tantrins not only played a significant role in supporting or dethroning Kashmiri kings, but also battled each other for influence and control over the land and its surplus. In need of resources, kings began to plunder Brahmanical institutions such as temples and temple endowments, leading to a severe weakening of these institutions, their spiritual hold, and their relationship to the agriculturally based economic system. This allowed for the concomitant growth of craft production and a search for new markets for craft products, which in turn led to an influx of traders from outside Kashmir (Hangloo 2000: 52–3). These trends gathered force as outside kingdoms began to intervene in the affairs of the weakening polity, and had reached a critical stage by the time Kalhana composed his historical poem in the mid-twelfth century.

The 8,000-verse *Rajatarangini* is divided into eight sections or books, and in the first few verses of the first book, Kalhana not only establishes himself as the poet-historian of Kashmir by naming his sources and commenting on them, but more significantly defines Kashmir as a sacred entity created through divine intervention. The origin story of Kashmir as told in these early verses of the first section is a distillation of numerous stories narrated in earlier narratives, including *Nilamata Purana*, and much like them draws on both universal Brahmanical ideas as well as local ideas drawn from Kashmir's regional cults.

According to this story, the land of Kashmir emerged from the lake Satisar, named after the goddess Sati, once it was drained at Sage Kashyap's instigation, to reveal and kill the demon Jalodbhava by Lord Vishnu. This land was protected by Nila, the lord of Nagas (serpent deities) and in turn protected them from Garuda (the mythical bird that hunted serpents) by stretching out its mountain walls around them. As the River Vitasta, Gauri (Sati, Shiva's consort) continued to make her home in this land. As Kumkum Roy notes, 'Kalhana locates Kashmir at the intersection of both unique and broad-based notions of sacred space', drawn from 'puranic cosmography and more specific local beliefs' (Roy 2003: 54).

Again, as in earlier narratives, Kashmir's geography and topography—and control over them—were essential to its definition as a privileged space. Its water bodies and mountains emerged as especially significant; while the former purified it and endowed it with sacredness, so that, as Kalhana writes, 'there is not a space as large as a grain of sesamum without a Tirtha', the latter formed a protective ring around it, so that it 'may be conquered by the force of spiritual merits, but not by forces of soldiers' (Stein 1979 [1900], vol. I: 9). Moreover, Kashmir's geographical location and physical features rendered it into a unique space, blessing it with a salubrious climate, rivalling, even perhaps surpassing, heaven in the things that could be found within its confines, such as learning, grapes, and icy water. While water gave birth to the land, it could also wreak havoc on it in the form of floods, a common occurrence in the latter parts of the narrative, which are given over to descriptions of political anarchy and moral lassitude, when the land could no longer lay claim to its sacred status.

For Kalhana, thus, as Shonaleeka Kaul argues, Kashmir was also defined as an ethical space. It was a space on which the narrative allowed even the kings portrayed as evil to endow temples, mathas, agraharas and other religious institutions that became pilgrimage sites, thus mirroring the sacredness of its physical landscape onto its built landscape. Moreover, a very specific list of qualities defined rulers as good versus evil, including their generosity towards and general treatment of their subjects, good conduct, and justness, among others (Kaul 2013: 220–1; see also Kaul 2018). While written to serve as a guide for kings, *Rajatarangini* nonetheless glorified their status and endowed them with the right to rule over their domain: 'Kasmir-land is Parvati; know that its king is a portion of Siva. Though he be wicked, a wise man who desires [his own] prosperity, will not despise him' (Stein 1979 [1900], vol. I: 14).

As opposed to its earlier sections, in which *Rajatarangini* crafts an idealized vision of Kashmir, the later sections present a more realistic picture of early medieval Kashmir in the recent past and contemporary period. As Roy points out, neighbouring kingdoms acquired a greater importance in later sections of the narrative, and rather than making grand conquests of faraway lands as in the early sections, Kashmir's rulers of the more recent past established control over neighbouring realms, such as Rajouri, Champa, and Lohara, through intermediaries. The rulers and people of these lands, in turn, participated in succession disputes to Kashmir's throne. Within Kashmir itself, there was a division between the regions to the north and south of Srinagar in the Vitasta Valley (Madavarajya and Kamarajya), with rebels taking refuge in and being backed by one of these regions. In the latter sections of *Rajatarangini*, thus, rather than being the paramount polity in the northern part of the subcontinent, Kashmir appears, in Roy's words, as part of 'a constellation of relatively small principalities whose aspiring and actual rulers constantly jostled for power and influence within their own realms as well as amongst their neighbors' (Roy 2003: 61–3).

In these sections, *Rajatarangini* makes a distinction between upholding the Brahmanical *varna* (caste) order that in many cases comes across as disintegrating, and consolidating control, which required rulers to carry out particular, sometimes unsavoury, administrative policies. These policies, particularly temple destruction, were designed to mobilize resources and prevent the consolidation of power and consequently rebellion amongst certain social groups, including mountain-dwellers, people in the countryside such as Damaras, and military groups such as Tantrins (Roy 2010: 150–1). Royal women and courtesans, many in positions of political and sexual power, make their appearance in later sections of the narrative in much greater numbers, in part reflecting the text's concerns with the disintegration of the ideal varna order in Kashmir. At the same time, they illustrate the power exercised by women as well as the flexibility of sexual relations as part of political strategy within the Kashmiri polity. Queens such as Sugandha and Didda, for instance, strengthened their authority by entering into relations with ministers (Roy 2010: 149). Another way in which royal women and other contenders to power registered their aspirations was by endowing religious institutions, in many cases of more than one sect (Roy 2010: 159–60).

In general, *Rajatarangini*'s later sections illustrate that the power of the king and the perfect moral order were under constant threat in early medieval Kashmir—from royal women, non-royal men, rebellions from within the kingdom, and rulers from neighbouring principalities. It is in this context that the narrative presents a carefully crafted vision of an ideal Kashmir located in a mythical past, universally celebrated, especially blessed, naturally protected from outsiders, and as Roy states, 'constituting the apex of the universe' with its rulers 'exercising universal sway' (Roy 2003: 55). It also reminds us of the backdrop for the forging of a new religio-political consensus in Kashmir.

Islamic Land

The durability of the idea of Kashmir as an auspicious and cosmographically central landscape is evident in its utilization in yet another project: that of Kashmir's transition to Islam. This project, again, was not merely religious, but rather a deeply political one that entailed the re-orientation of the very polity of Kashmir towards the Islamic world. Moreover, as earlier, it encapsulated an interconnectedness between the narrative and political traditions, and was located at the intersection of universal assertions and local ideas. Kashmir emerged out of this project as a sanctified, purified space especially suitable for conversion to Islam, which allowed it to claim its rightful place at the centre of the Islamic world. Not surprisingly, the narratives that articulated this project were written in yet another chaotic period in Kashmir's history—the second half of the sixteenth century—when the Kashmiri Sultanate, the political manifestation of Kashmir's successful transition to Islam, had declined.

The Kashmiri Sultanate (1343–1556) emerged from the crisis of the fourteenth-century Kashmiri polity—long in the making—that was unable to control internal rebellions and outside attacks, such as those by the Mongol general Zulju in 1320. This allowed a military general from Swat, Shah Mir, to eventually

13

take control of the throne as Sultan Shamsuddin. However, it was not until Sultan Qutubuddin (r. 1373–89) ascended to the throne that Islam came to acquire state patronage. At this time, the Kubrawi Sufi master and saint Sayyid Ali Hamadani made his way to Kashmir from Hamadan in Persia—allegedly fleeing Timur's persecutions—accompanied by his followers and their families. Hamadani attained the favour of the sultan, who, in the tradition of earlier Kashmiri monarchs, offered him and his followers revenue-free land grants for maintenance and accorded them with high positions within the court.

The sultan's son and successor, Sultan Sikandar (r. 1389–1413), has to be credited with consolidating Islam as a political and religious force in Kashmir. He attacked Brahmanical control by demolishing temples and agraharas (a process, it must be noted here, begun by his 'Hindu' predecessors), instead patronizing the building of shrines (*khanqah*s or *ziarat*s) commemorating Sufi mystics on the Kashmiri landscape, the most significant among them the shrine dedicated to the memory of Sayyid Ali Hamadani in Srinagar. In many cases, temples were transformed to mosques and shrines by the people themselves, who were converting in large numbers to Islam, attracted to the new, more egalitarian, way of life being presented to them through the activities of Sufi masters, Sayyids, and their disciples. Moreover, local ascetic groups such as the Rishis and individuals such as Lal Ded were drawn to the new ideas circulating in Kashmir, encouraging their acceptance among the people as a means to attain a better life (Hangloo 2000: 56–9).

At the Sultanate's height, the kingdom of Kashmir included Ladakh, Baltistan, Rajouri, Poonch, Kishtwar, and other neighbouring principalities that had separated from the kingdom with the collapse of the central authority in early medieval Kashmir (Mattoo 1988: 95). Furthermore, migrations of Turks, Persians, and Central Asians into Kashmir, encouraged by Sultan Sikandar in the context of Timur's invasion of India in 1398, led to the introduction of new artisanal skills, which provided work to the locals and increased trade and intellectual relations between Central Asia and Kashmir.

Alongside Kashmiri traders, who travelled in increasing numbers to Central Asia and beyond, Kashmiri scholars travelled to the famed Sufi centres and madrasas of Samarkand and Bukhara to study Islamic jurisprudence, theology, and Persian poetry (Bamzai 1980: 217). Economic changes pushed people towards towns, thereby breaking down the hold of groups such as Brahmans and Damaras over them (Hangloo 2000: 58–9). Urban shrines in particular became centres of spiritual, economic, and literary activities, gradually extending their reach amongst the populace while at the same time legitimizing the authority of the Sultanate. By the early fifteenth century, most of Kashmir's population, including a substantial section of Brahmans, had converted to Islam, and Persian was increasingly becoming the language of the literate classes.

Nevertheless, Sanskrit and Persian coexisted on Kashmir's intellectual landscape through the sixteenth century, drawing copiously on each other's literary repertoires. Both languages flourished in the court of the Kashmiri sultan Zain-ul-Abidin (r. 1420–70), a moment in Kashmir's history characterized, according to Satoshi Ogura (2015), by 'linguistic cosmopolitanism'. The sultan patronized the languages equally, and under his direction, several Sanskrit narratives, including *Mahabharata*, were translated into Persian, and Persian narratives, such as Abd Al-Rahman Jami's *Yusuf Zuliekha*, into Sanskrit. The Sultan's court poets continued the narrative tradition of Kalhana's *Rajatarangini*; in *Jainatarangini* (begun in 1459), for instance, Srivara introduced new elements to Sanskrit composition that were deeply infused with the Islamic idiom and described his patron's rule as restoring Kashmir to its status as paradise on earth (Inden 2008: 548; Obrock 2013). At the same time, he himself recognized the growing significance of Persian on the literary landscape of Kashmir, describing it as *desa*, or native literature (Pollock 2012: 419fn12). As a cosmopolitan language that took on a vernacular idiom in Kashmir, Persian was thus well-suited to the project of bringing together the universal and local in crystallizing the idea of Kashmir as a sacred space blessed by Islam.

Kashmir's Persian literary tradition consisted primarily of two kinds of narratives—*tazkira*s (hagiographies) of the Sufi saints of Kashmir and *tarikh*s (traditional histories). However, the line between these narratives was often blurred, with tazkiras recounting the political past and tarikhs detailing the lives and deeds of Sufi saints. The authors of these narratives were associated more often with Sufi shrines than with the royal court, and as a result the narratives circulated widely among the literate and non-literate alike, attesting further to their vernacularity. The narratives and the stories associated with them naturalized both Islam, and Persian itself, onto Kashmir's landscape by selectively drawing on Kashmir's earlier narrative tradition while blending it into the Islamic imagination. The influence wielded by these narratives, therefore, was immense, made more significant by the fact that the institutions that supported the production of these narratives—Sufi shrines—had become immensely powerful corporatized institutions by the sixteenth century.

By the early sixteenth century, Kashmir was home to numerous Sufi sects, including the Suhrawardiya, Kubrawiya, Nurbakhshiya, and Naqshbandiya, each of which controlled vast lands and resources through shrines that dotted Kashmir's landscape and competed with each other for religious and political influence. The Sultanate's authority had begun to gradually decline after the death of Sultan Zain-ul-Abidin in 1470, in part due to the Sultan's own inability to resolve the succession struggle between his two sons before his death, as well as the entry of the Baihaqi Sayyids (originally from Khorasan but settled in Delhi) into Kashmir's political landscape once the sultan entered into matrimonial relations with them.

The politics of shrines, so closely associated with the powerful, became the focal point for the ensuing struggle for power among the Sayyids and Kashmir's noble clans, which came to a crescendo in the first half of the sixteenth century. The jostling among groups of nobles and their associates, as well as interference from neighbouring hill-states that had fallen from Sultanate control, finally led to the end of the Sultanate in 1556, followed by further chaos as the Chak family of nobles took over Kashmir's throne. Only nominally in power, the Chaks were unable to restore the stability of Kashmir's central authority, which was under constant threat from within and without its frontiers.

Since the political institution that represented Islam in Kashmir appeared to be in grave jeopardy, and the relationships among Sufi sects, their khanqahs, the royal court, and other emergent centres of power were not entirely clear, the narrative rendering of Kashmir as an ideal Islamic landscape became especially paramount. The competing narratives thus attempted to clarify the relationships amongst these political and spiritual entities in the present by focusing on the history of the spread of Islam in Kashmir, especially through the activities of particular Sufi orders, their preceptors, and followers. The efforts of these Sufi sects to convert the landscape of Kashmir to Islam was closely tied in these narratives to the triumph of the Kashmiri Sultanate, with at least some of its sultans embodying an ideal kingship.

The ultimate objective of the authors of these narratives—most of whom were either managers of, or otherwise closely associated with, particular shrines—was to intervene in the political discourse of sixteenth-century Kashmir by asserting the claims of specific religio-political groups over others to particular sacred spaces, and through them, to political power over Kashmir the sacred land itself.[2]

The past deeds of powerful Sufi teachers and guides, such as Sayyid Ali Hamadani and Sheikh Hamza Makdoom, to transform Kashmir into an Islamic space formed the centrepiece of these narratives. Much like earlier Sanskrit narratives, the Persian tradition too drew on universal and regional ideas simultaneously to assert its claims and reorient Kashmir as an Islamic

19

space with links to lands further west, in Central Asia and Persia, such as Khuttlan, Hamadan, and Herat. At the same time, the tradition attempted to localize Islam by associating it with the indigenous mystical sect of the Rishis of Kashmir (Zutshi 2014).

In presenting Kashmir as spiritually and politically perfect in the relatively recent past, this narrative tradition reflected the deep divisions that characterized the Kashmiri polity throughout the sixteenth century. Beginning in the late fifteenth century, Kashmiri sultans began to play a variety of Sayyid and non-Sayyid groups of nobles—such as Chaks, Magareys, Chadurahs, and Baihaqis—and associated Sufi sects against each other in an attempt to consolidate their power. The excessive exemptions, concessions, and donations by the sultans to these groups had undermined the socio-economic and political structure to a point where by the third decade of the sixteenth century, not only was food scarcity common but these groups competed fiercely, sometimes in collusion with outside forces, to install and dethrone Kashmir's rulers (Hangloo 2000: 108–9).

The rulers were no longer able to control Kashmir's centre or its peripheries, losing territory in the process and setting the stage for the Mughal conquest. Towards the end of the sixteenth century, rulers such as Yusuf Shah Chak turned against certain sections of their own population (Sunnis) in an attempt to consolidate power.

In the case of Yusuf Shah, this led to a revolt against his authority by several Sunni elders, who helped Mughal forces to conquer Kashmir. While the Persian narrative tradition blamed this political chaos on the absence of rightly guided Sufi mystics in Kashmir, it was in fact Sufi mystics themselves, as well as the shrines that they controlled, that played a central role in the crisis of the sixteenth-century Kashmiri polity.

Paradise on Earth

The idea of Kashmir as sacred space took on renewed meaning with the incorporation of Kashmir into the Mughal Empire in 1585–6. During the Mughal period, Kashmir's indigenous Sanskrit and Persian traditions converged with the Mughal imperial tradition to reassert the idea of Kashmir as a paradise on earth, this time remade by god's instrument on earth himself—the Mughal emperor. This idea was expressed, as earlier, through narratives and building activities, and was tied to the massive political transition of Kashmir from an independent kingdom to a constituent part of a subcontinental empire. It was a significant means of validating the Mughal conquest of Kashmir when Mughal forces were facing rebellions across the region and of fortifying Mughal presence once relative peace had been restored.

Modern Kashmiri historiography often portrays the Mughal association with Kashmir, largely due to contemporary political imperatives, as an unqualified conquest, with the submission, if not complete erasure, of Kashmiri ideas, traditions, and institutions (Hassnain 2009: 6–36). In reality the relationship between the Mughals and Kashmir was far more complicated, mediated through negotiations among Mughal rulers, their agents, and certain sections of the Kashmiri population. Kashmir did indeed lose political independence to the Mughal Empire, which rendered it into a territorial/administrative unit (*sarkar*) harnessed to the political economy of the empire, endowing the space with a symbolic coherence through architectural and narrative practices. However, Kashmiris themselves were not simply oppressed bystanders in this process; rather, they continually asserted their right to define Kashmir and its relationship to the Mughal Empire.

Even the most vehement critics of the Mughals would grudgingly admit that the onset of Mughal governance in late sixteenth-century Kashmir settled the disordered political situation by quelling sectarian divisions and pacifying the warring nobility in a number of ways, including by integrating them into the new Mughal administrative system, intermarriage, and banishment for the most recalcitrant. The Chak nobles who were not banished to other parts of the Mughal

Empire found refuge with the rulers of Kishtwar until the principality was brought under Mughal control in the 1620s, followed by Ladakh, Baltistan, and other adjacent hill-states (Mattoo 1988: 29–31).

Agriculture was restored as peasants returned to their abandoned lands and more land was brought under cultivation, especially as orchards, even as land revenue collection was streamlined (Parmu 1969: 289–91; Mattoo 1988: 42–6). Kashmir's economy was thus revived by being drawn into the subcontinental system of agriculture, trade, and commerce, which created new administrative and social groups, such as *muqadam*s and *mansabdar*s, as well as new trading classes, such as shawl merchants. These groups were in favour of continuing and fostering the relationship with the empire that afforded them opportunities for upward mobility. Ruling Kashmir largely through their governors (*subahdar*s), the Mughal emperors nevertheless displayed an unusual interest in the region—evident in their periodic visits—because of its position as the summer capital of the empire (Mattoo 1988: 100).

Abul Fazl's *Ain-i-Akbari* best encapsulates the ways in which Kashmir's indigenous narrative tradition, and through it Kashmir, was seamlessly appropriated into the Mughal imperial imagination. *Ain-i-Akbari* draws a direct line of descent from Kalhana's *Rajatarangini* and its continuations, at the same time establishing Akbar as the rightful culmination of kingship in Kashmir:

> When the Imperial standards were for the first time borne aloft in this garden of perpetual spring, a book called *Raj Tarangini* written in the Sanskrit tongue containing an account of the princes of Kashmir during a period of some four thousand years, was presented to his Majesty. (Fazl 2004, vol. II: 844)

He, thus, recognized Kashmir as a kingdom with a distinct history and an interconnected narrative tradition that recorded it, with both region and tradition now integral to the larger historical narrative of the Mughal Empire.

It is in its descriptions of Kashmir, the land, however, that *Ain* echoes and extends Kashmir's indigenous tradition. Kashmir was not simply a territory and administrative unit of the Mughal Empire—a sarkar in the *subah* (province) of Kabul that also comprised Pakhli, Bhimbar, Swat, Bajaur, Qandahar, and Zabulistan—but equally significantly, it was also 'a garden of perpetual spring surrounding a citadel terraced to the skies, and deservedly appropriate to be either the delight of the worldling or the retired abode of the recluse' (Fazl 2004, vol. II: 829–31). Thus, it was both a worldly and spiritual paradise replete with enchanting flowers, juicy fruits, and pilgrimage sites, many of which, much like *Nilamata Purana*, Fazl describes at length. The recognition of the special qualities of Kashmir's landscape was a means for the Mughals to gain spiritual merit by associating with the land, rather than claiming it simply as a territory.

As Kashmir became a summer retreat for the Mughal royalty, its landscape was adorned to fit the appellation of paradise on earth through construction projects. There was a particularly imperial bent to these projects that aimed to seamlessly incorporate Kashmir into the Mughal imperial imaginary, while rendering it into a more pleasurable refuge—a 'garden of delights'—from the searing heat of the north Indian plains. Jahangir, who had a special affinity with Kashmir, spent eight summers in the Valley and is responsible for some of the most beautiful garden projects there, including the Shalimar Bagh overlooking the Dal Lake, with the Zabarwan mountains as its backdrop (Asher 1992: 124–5; Michell 2011: 313–14). Significantly, most Mughal architecture in Kashmir was constructed in stone rather than wood to distinguish the imperial aesthetic from local mosque and shrine architecture as well as to suggest the permanence of the empire (Hamdani 2016: 2).

Kashmir's beautiful landscape, rendered thus through these construction projects, was then commemorated in poetic assemblies organized during the visits of the emperors and royal governors, in which Iranian, Mughal, and Kashmiri poets competed with each other. Kashmiri poet Muhammad Aslam 'Salim' (d. 1718), celebrated Jahangir's achievement in constructing Shalimar thus:

> Once such a great monarch became its architect,
> Shalimar gained many a charm:
>
> Canals, falls, ponds and fountains,
> trees, flower beds, buildings and sheds;
>
> Thus a Heaven was created on the earth,
> the like of which was never seen before. (Tikku 1971: 98–9)

Although cast in Indo-Persian literary styles, Kashmiri poets drew as much on the indigenous narrative tradition to define Kashmir as a sacred space with natural defenses that had to be won by the force of merit rather than force alone.

A similar trend is visible in the Kashmiri histories composed during the Mughal period, which while drawing on Mughal texts such as *Ain*, remained firmly located within the indigenous narrative tradition. These narratives reclaimed the space of Kashmir from the Mughal imperial imagination by asserting its singularity, evident in its local past and its independent association with the Islamic world. Despite being written when the author was serving as Jahangir's governor in Kashmir, *Tarikh-i Haider Malik* (1620–1)—a history of Kashmir by Haider Malik Chadurah—asserts Kashmir's distinctiveness in a number of ways (Zutshi 2014: 93–6).

The incorporation of Kashmir into the Mughal Empire—and the resultant movement of people and goods—allowed for an intense cross-fertilization of ideas between Kashmir and the Indo-Persian world, which gave birth to a literary culture that drew on new trends while at the same time remaining anchored to the indigenous narrative tradition. Kashmir was a paradise on earth, even perhaps an imperial paradise, but what rendered it such was its sacred landscape, made so by its natural attributes and pilgrimage spots, and by the traversals of its holy figures and mystics. So powerful was this idea of Kashmir as an auspicious landscape that it allowed Kashmir to retain its individuality and autonomy even in the face of its incorporation into the mighty Mughal Empire.

This chapter, thus, illustrates that Kashmir's religio-political and textual landscapes were intimately connected, and the idea of Kashmir as sacred space—created and so evocatively articulated in its multilingual narrative tradition—allowed Kashmir's rulers and other groups to assert a centrality for this polity. As significantly, it cemented the partnership between ruling and religious groups for the maintenance of a socio-economic order, with the former endowing religious institutions, while the latter endowed rulers with the right to rule and channelled the land's resources towards the central authority. Critical as the idea was to the success of several political, economic and spiritual projects, it was endlessly replicated and took on varied forms throughout the history of Kashmir.

The chapter also makes clear that Kashmir has never been an isolated realm on the frontier—it has drawn on, and attempted to draw in, the outside world, including its more immediate neighbours as well as places farther afield, such as Central Asia and even China. And much like the rest of the subcontinent, or indeed many other parts of the world, it is a palimpsest of multiple religious, political, and linguistic traditions, which have at times co-existed, at other times deeply influenced each other, at yet other times been at odds, and which continue to define its tumultuous present.

Notes

1. Ghai (1973, vol. 2: 7).
2. For a longer discussion, see Zutshi (2014: ch. 1).

2

Kashmir as *Mulk*

God wanted that this blue-colored land
Should tire of wailing like the reed's heart.

He gave its control to the Afghan,
He gave Jamshid's garden to the demons.

—Anonymous[1]

This anonymous verse, which was often recited by
Kashmiris during the Afghan period (1753–1819),
captures the sea change in Kashmir's political situation
and the corresponding shifts within its narrative tradition
in the eighteenth century. From the celebrations of
Kashmir's beauty, sacredness, and the land's geographical
and symbolic centrality to larger political entities and
spiritual projects, Kashmir's narrative tradition shifted
to mourning the holy land's systematic destruction.
Through these jeremiads, however, emerged the idea

of Kashmir as a homeland (*mulk*)—a space that had to be protected from the depredations of outsiders by gaining control of and recounting its past—and its people as a distinct group—a *quom*. This chapter follows the emergence of the ideas of mulk and quom on Kashmir's narrative landscape, both powerful symbols of rebellion for the inhabitants of Kashmir, who used them to assert their regional identity in the face of the loss of political and economic power. Thus, while still deeply political, and to an extent also located at the intersection of the universal and local, these ideas rebelled against rather than validating larger imperial and other projects.

The Long Eighteenth Century

Despite its significance, there are hardly any studies of eighteenth-century Kashmir, a period that appears to get lost between the Mughal period (itself hardly written about) and the creation of the princely state of Jammu and Kashmir in the mid-nineteenth century. Much like in the rest of the subcontinent, the eighteenth century was a moment of crisis and tremendous transformation in Kashmir. As the Mughal Empire began its long slide into decline and retreat after Aurangzeb's death in 1707, its impact was deeply felt in Kashmir in a variety of ways, including in the near-breakdown of the centralized administrative apparatus, attacks from frontier tribes, the re-emergence of sectarian conflicts, the establishment and strengthening of particular social classes, and devastating floods and famines, eventually leading to the incorporation of Kashmir into the Afghan Empire, to be followed by the Sikh Kingdom.

The disorder and chaos of the Mughal court in the first half of the eighteenth century played itself out in Kashmir as the governorship of the sarkar changed hands 57 times in 46 years. Since the governors changed so often, deputy governors, many of them local Kashmiris, came to acquire important positions within the administration. In the absence of the check of the imperial court—communications with which were severely disrupted due to revolts and conflict across Mughal territories, especially the Punjab—the well-ordered administrative apparatus laid down by earlier Mughal emperors and their governors frayed at the seams, with oppressive taxation, lawlessness, and food shortages increasingly burdening the people.

Since their power was so tenuous, many governors, deputy governors, and their associates encouraged sectarian divisions to maintain their control. These divisions played along the familiar lines of Shia–Sunni–Pandit as in other parts of the disintegrating Mughal Empire, with Kashmiri Pandits—a social

31

class that had coalesced by the end of the seventeenth century and held significant positions in the Mughal administration—being targeted in the new dispensation. The majority Sunni and the minority Shia populations of Kashmir, both linked to major Sufi orders such as the Kubrawiya and Nurbhakshiya respectively, had always been in competition over shrines and followers. In the eighteenth century, Shia–Sunni tensions heightened as socio-political conditions deteriorated, and in a series of incidents that began with the persecution of Pandits by the Qazi of Srinagar in 1720, for instance, Shias were blamed for joining hands with Pandits against Sunnis (Parmu 1969: 339–42).

These anarchic conditions resulting from the collapse of the governmental system were exacerbated by the attacks of frontier hill tribes, known as the Khakhas and Bombas, on the Valley. The weakness of the Mughal Empire led to the declaration of independence by hill tribes, followed by looting raids, and even the acquisition of territories in and around Kashmir. In certain instances, the governors and deputy governors allied with the Khakha and Bomba chiefs of Muzaffarabad and Karna, and the Gujjars of Poonch to strengthen their power, allowing them to plunder in exchange for military support, which ultimately led to Kashmiris rising in revolt against both the deputy governors and the hill tribesmen (Parmu 1969: 343–5).

Portrayed in contemporary narratives and modern scholarly literature as unruly nomadic plunderers from the frontier that needed to be disciplined by the state centred in the Kashmir Valley (not unlike the portrayal of Damaras in *Rajatarangini*), these groups represent the constantly shifting relationship between the centres of power in the Valley and its surrounding lands, as well as their inhabitants.

By the 1730s, then, the frontier lands of the lower Jhelum Valley and Poonch were once again determining the fate of the Valley and its people, as the internecine battles among imperial, provincial, and local notables for control increasingly characterized its polity. Widespread maladministration and penury ensued, intensified by the floods and resultant famines that stalked Kashmir in the 1740s, wiping out more than three quarters of its population through starvation, disease, and emigration (Bamzai 1962: 383). Kashmir was, thus, ripe for the picking in the much larger ongoing contest for the control of northwestern India among the Mughals, Afghans, Marathas, and Sikhs. As the Afghans emerged victorious in this contest, the squabbles within Kashmir's administration increased, with one side inviting the Afghan ruler, Ahmad Shah Abdali, to send Afghan forces to take over Kashmir. In 1753, after a bloody two-week battle, Kashmir became part of the Afghan Empire.

Afghan rule, which officially ended in 1819, did not substantially change the trends that had characterized the political and social landscapes of Kashmir in the first half of the eighteenth century; rather, it exacerbated them. Caught between several emergent and warring kingdoms and empires, Kashmir remained at the mercy of a series of Afghan governors, a few of whom rebelled against their Afghan overlords by seeking support from the Mughals and Sikhs. For instance, Sukh Jeewan Mal, a Punjabi Khattri born in Kabul, became the Afghan governor of Kashmir in 1753, and utilized the retreat of the Afghans from the Punjab to declare his allegiance to the Mughal emperor, Alamgir II, who bestowed on him the title of Raja; he ruled Kashmir until 1762, when he was dethroned and the Afghans retook control of Kashmir.

The burden of heavy taxation on all social classes became heavier still; cleavages between sects and religious groups widened, sometimes encouraged by the governors; and the hill-tribes continued their pillaging raids on the Valley whenever the administration seemed weak, leaving behind a trail of destruction, starvation, and deaths (Parmu 1969: 351–3).

Nevertheless, Afghan rule did bring new opportunities for merchants and other social groups as a result of the establishment of more direct trade and other links between Kashmir, Kabul, Peshawar, and lands further west. It is interesting to note that although some Afghan governors targeted the Hindu population of Kashmir for particular local reasons, as a whole, Kashmiri Pandits emerged as indispensable administrators, revenue collectors, diplomats, and literary figures during Afghan rule (Parmu 1969: 352; Tikku 1971: 166; Koul 1991 [1924]: 19).[2] Kashmiri Pandits had become a part of the 'socio-linguistic complex of Persian' (see Alam and Subrahmanyam 2004), and a significant scribal class as early as the Sultanate period—forming a bridge among the worlds of Sanskrit, Persian, and Kashmiri—a position that was expanded under the Mughals, and consolidated in the context of Kashmir's incorporation into the Afghan Empire.

Given their increasing significance, it is not surprising that it was Kashmiri Pandit *karkun* (scribes/ administrators), sensing the decline of Afghan authority and the emergence of the Sikhs as a major power in northwestern India, who facilitated Kashmir's incorporation into the Sikh Kingdom. This transition, however, has to be located in the much broader context of Ranjit Singh's ambitions as well as the advance of three imperial powers in the early nineteenth century— British India, Tsarist Russia, and Qing China—and the contest amongst them for gaining influence over Central Asia to maintain their own empires. Kashmir, located as it was at the crossroads of these imperial entities, acquired an invaluable strategic significance in this context.

For Ranjit Singh, the Sikh ruler, control of Kashmir was essential to obtaining and maintaining his dream of hegemony north of the River Sutlej, since he could not extend territorial control south of the river as per his agreement with the British Indian government. Although Sikh armies finally wrested control of Kashmir from the Afghans in 1819, colonial influence in the region grew steadily through the activities of spies, traders, scientists, missionaries, and other such agents (Bamzai 1962: 553–4, 563–4).

Sikh rule was not qualitatively different than Afghan rule in terms of administration, revenue collection, and so on. Ranjit Singh left the administration of Kashmir to his governors, many of whom were Punjabi Khattris and took control of its administrative machinery with the help of Kashmiri karkun. Since Ranjit Singh was engaged in near-constant warfare like the Afghans, taxes continued to be oppressive, and in an attempt to increase revenues even further, the Sikh administration resumed *jagir*s (land grants) that had been held by Muslim families and shrines since the Mughal period, while at the same time endowing other land grants, some revenue-free, to non-Muslims.

Moreover, as a result of their previous experiences in Muslim territories, Sikh governors undertook several policies aimed specifically at Muslims with the objective of tamping down Muslim opposition; however, these policies—such as the ban on cow slaughter and *azan* (Muslim call to prayer); closing down of the Jama Masjid for public prayer; and the seizure of other mosques as property of the state—served to alienate the Muslim population. *Begar* (forced labour), imposed by the Sikh administration to facilitate the supply of materials to their armies; the poor working conditions of weavers as the shawl trade flourished, which at the same time enriched shawl merchants; and several famines in the 1830s added to the woes of the people (Bamzai 1962: 561–71).

When Sikh rule finally came to an end in 1846, Kashmir had changed hands between several imperial entities within a century and a half. Its inhabitants had borne the brunt of the policies undertaken by these regimes, which at best displayed a benign neglect towards them or at worst fleeced them, all in the service of larger imperial interests. Nevertheless, certain groups, both Muslim and Hindu, benefited as a result due to increased access to political and economic resources, and a transformed narrative tradition re-asserted the idea of Kashmir as an autonomous entity, if not in political then at least in symbolic terms.

Defining *Mulk-i-Kashmir* and the *Quom*

The political conditions that characterized the long eighteenth century encouraged the articulation of the idea of Kashmir as homeland within Kashmir's narrative tradition, which flourished in this period despite lack of political patronage. Continuing to draw on universal and local ideas, writers nevertheless looked inward in an attempt to make sense of the prevailing conditions in Kashmir. Some of the authors of these narratives were linked to the administration, but most were connected to shrines and Sufi sects, for whom the eighteenth century was a moment of acute crisis. Not only had their relationship to the political authority crumbled over the course of the eighteenth century, but by the early nineteenth century, Islam as a whole seemed to be under threat in Kashmir. The only way to preserve Kashmir as *Bagh-i-Suleiman* (Garden of Solomon) was by claiming it as a distinct mulk, a region—not merely a place or an administrative unit—whose distinctiveness was apparent in its past and the tradition of recording that past. It was in the continuation of that tradition that despite the ravages on its landscape, Kashmir could assert its regional identity as a place especially blessed by the divine.

Regional identities emerged across the subcontinent in the wake of the Mughal decline and the establishment of independent kingdoms in the eighteenth century. In some cases, such as the Maratha and Sikh kingdoms, for instance, these identities were fostered by the ruling power through a common language, religion, and ideological and actual battles with 'others' that were memorialized for future generations (Bayly 1998: 21). In Kashmir, on the other hand, it was its incorporation into larger empires and kingdoms—and the resultant political and economic dislocation—that encouraged a sense of belonging to a region and its expression in the cosmopolitan vernacular, Persian. The rulers themselves became the greatest 'others' within this tradition, their tyrannies on the land and its people forever inscribed, never to be forgotten. Moreover, sectarian affiliations came into sharper focus within the narrative tradition as it focused on what it meant to be Kashmiri.

Kashmir as the Valley thus emerged in these narratives as a mulk set apart from other mulks through its special characteristics as well as its geographical location, capable of standing on its own rather than as part of larger Brahmanical, Islamic, or Mughal worlds. Most significantly, the assertion of the mulk's uniqueness lay in its historical tradition, of which these narratives claimed to be continuations. History as embodied in the historical narrative, both as a tradition of recording the past and as facts about the past, gave shape and voice to the mulk. So intimately tied were the two that, in a sense, the narratives became Kashmir. In significant ways, eighteenth-century narratives were regional histories painting a vivid picture of conditions specific to Kashmir's recent past and present (see Zutshi 2014: ch. 2).

Late eighteenth-century narratives began to focus further on the category of people—the inhabitants of this mulk or the quom. They focused on the widespread desolation, dishonesty, tyranny, and misrule within the mulk—resembling *qayamat* (apocalypse)—occasioned by the advent of Afghan rule, relating the policies of successive Afghan governors as cruel and inhumane, which ruined trade, bankrupted shopkeepers, reduced peasants to penury, and created famine. While the genealogy of the land was important—and the narratives rehearse the familiar tale of Kashmir's creation through divine intervention—the genealogy of its people was equally significant, thus creating the idea of 'Kashmiri', an inhabitant of the Valley. The sectarian underpinnings of the Kashmiri quom, moreover, were more sharply defined in these narratives, especially between Shia and Sunni (Zutshi 2014: ch. 2).

Narrating *Mulk* and *Quom* in the Regional Vernacular

Even as Persian prose and poetry continued to articulate the deep sense of love and loss for the homeland, attesting to and contributing towards an emergent regional identity, the regional vernacular, Kashmiri, which had until that moment remained a largely oral language, came into its own at the turn of the nineteenth century. This has to be located in the context of the more general trend in the subcontinent towards regional vernaculars, such as Hindavi/Urdu, which emerged in the wake of Mughal decline. The trend, which illustrated the rise of regional idioms in response to the Persianized culture of the Mughal court, led to a feverish interaction between the Persian textual and Kashmiri oral traditions, especially since the latter came to be written in the Persian script starting in the latter half of the eighteenth century. For its part, Persian was deeply influenced by its transactions with Kashmiri, and later Urdu, oral and literary traditions.

Although the Afghans and the Sikhs did not patronize Kashmiri, or for that matter Persian, literary production, low-level administrators, *pir*s (religious elders), and Sufi poets began to compose a variety of verse, recording it in the Persian script, thus leading to Kashmiri's revival as a written language. Much of this writing, usually by minor religious figures (pirs and hakims, for instance), consisted of translations of Persian classics into Kashmiri, such as Jami's *Yusuf Zulaikha* and Firdausi's *Shahnama*; folk stories from Kashmiri, Sanskrit, and Persian textual and oral traditions recast

41

anew; and renditions of religious topics from the history of Islam, or Hindu texts such as Ramayana. In most cases, this poetry drew on Kashmiri folk styles and forms of narration (such as the Kashmiri songs *vakhun*, *chakri*, and *roph*), thereby allowing it to be performed and thus circulated widely amongst the people. Moreover, this was the moment when Lal Ded's *vaakh*s and Nund Rishi's *shruk*s, considered the earliest forms of Kashmiri verse, were collected, recorded, and some also translated into Persian. For instance, collections of Nund Rishis's verses known as *Noornama*s, previously the sole domain of the caretakers of his shrine at Chrar Sharif, became more widely available in manuscript form (Zutshi 2014: 136–7).

Another characteristic of Kashmiri verse from this period that rendered it into a specifically regional poetry and a vehicle for a regional identity was that it embodied a profound sense of place. This was true not just of verse renditions of Kashmiri tales, but also of Kashmiri translations of Persian classics, which were recast to fit the Kashmiri landscape and local ideas and customs. Moreover, Kashmiri verse spoke to the concerns of the common people, and by the middle of the nineteenth century, had become a powerful means of protest against the tyrannies of rulers and their agents. And finally, it was in Kashmiri poetry that narrow sectarian affiliations could be bridged, transcended, and even accommodated in the interest of articulating a more inclusive regional identity against the outsiders bent on destroying the homeland. Drawing on past textual, oral, and mystical traditions in multiple languages, thus, Kashmiri verse maintained the idea of Kashmir as sacred space, giving people themselves, regardless of religious affiliation, a voice in its articulation.

The multiple renditions and trajectory of the story Himal–Nagaray capture perfectly the articulation of this deep sense of place at the intersection of Persian and Kashmiri textual, oral, and performance traditions. Although the story had been circulating in the oral sphere for centuries and was even mentioned in several Persian narratives, it is significant that it was rendered into Persian and Kashmiri verse several times in the eighteenth and nineteenth centuries—into Persian in the early eighteenth century, 1806, and 1821, and into Kashmiri in the 1840s and 1865, not to mention the countless times it was performed by storytellers— attesting to its resonance for the time period. During a time of discord, this story about the travails of the princess Himal and her lover Nagaray reminded people of what was still possible in Kashmir—love across social and religious barriers amidst a quintessentially pure landscape.

In some versions of the story, Himal is a princess and her lover Nagaray, a Naga who has taken the form of a person, is a poor Brahman's adopted son, while in others, Himal is identified as a Hindu princess and Nagaray as her Muslim lover. Not only does Himal lose Nagaray to water (a spring), which is his abode as a Naga, but the lovers are reunited at the end through the intervention of Shiva and Parvati, who bring about their final resurrection by immersing their ashes in the spring of eternal life. Water remerges as a powerful trope, capable of giving birth to land and threatening its submergence, thereby rehearsing Kashmir's very divine origins from water and celebrating its many sacred springs as essential to its identity.

These tellings and retellings of the story, and many other such stories of conflict and co-existence between different groups, offered social commentary by inviting the audience to participate in divine and social crossings, and if only momentarily, making it possible for the rich and poor, Hindu and Muslim, Shia and Sunni, to forget their differences and commemorate the land that made these crossings possible (Zutshi 2014: 280–5).

This chapter thus illustrates that the long eighteenth century brought many changes to Kashmir; as the centralized administration steadily eroded in the wake of the Mughal withdrawal, the compact between political and religious authority that had produced and sustained the idea of Kashmir as a sacred space par excellence unravelled with it. The incorporation of Kashmir into the Afghan Empire, followed by the Sikh Kingdom, led to a further onslaught on Kashmir's administrative and spiritual institutions, as taxation increased exponentially and revenue-free land grants were resumed and redistributed.

The common people continued to live under the yoke of poverty, forced labour, and many migrated from Kashmir to escape starvation. The result was a turn towards the idea of Kashmir as mulk within its Persian narrative tradition as the emergent elites as well as Sufi scholars associated with numerous embattled shrines patronized this tradition. These narratives eulogized the decline of Kashmir from a paradise on earth to an inferno of political and natural disasters. Kashmir was now clearly identified as the Valley, a homeland, and a distinct country that could not merely be appropriated into the universal geographies of Brahmanism, Islam, or the Mughal imperium.

Notes

1. Tikku (1971: 159).
2. Kashmiri Pandits were the descendants of the upper-caste Brahman Hindu families who had not converted to Islam during the Sultanate period. Instead, they acquired knowledge of Persian and worked within the Sultanate administration.

3

Kashmir as Princely State

Something strange has happened to these times,
Nothing is in its right place, whether ordinary
or important.
People leave the real and follow the superficial,
Nobody follows the laws of the *shariat*.
All of a sudden religious values have disappeared,
Whatever is against religion becomes the
law of the land.

—Maqbool Shah Kraalwari[1]

Maqbool Shah Kraalwari's *Pirnama* captures the alarm gripping the inhabitants of the Kashmir Valley as it underwent extraordinary transformations in the latter half of the nineteenth century. With the creation of the princely state of Jammu and Kashmir in 1846 by the British East India Company, the Valley became a constituent part of two imperial entities—the princely state with Gulab Singh's Dogra dynasty at the helm and the British Indian Empire. As the Dogras consolidated and validated their power over the state in the context of the looming British colonial presence and its interests, Kashmiris responded to their position as twice-removed colonial subjects by organizing into communities to define their identities and eventually to negotiate for their interests.

Islam—which until the eighteenth century had maintained a close relationship to the ruling power—now became the focal point of opposition to the state and its policies as Kashmir's public discourse was pervaded by a crescendo of voices debating and demarcating the contours of the Kashmiri Muslim community. And yet, its narrative tradition continued to memorialize Kashmir as an especially blessed landscape created and maintained through interactions among different religions, languages, and people.

Fashioning Jammu and Kashmir

The processes that culminated in the Treaty of Amritsar that founded Jammu and Kashmir and handed it over to the Dogra dynasty had begun in the early nineteenth century with the incorporation of Kashmir into the Sikh Kingdom in 1819. By this time, Kashmir was not only crucial to Sikh control over its territories, but was also emerging as strategically significant in the three-way contest among the British, Russian, and Chinese over the control of Central Asia. In addition, Gulab Singh, who had been granted the title of Raja and the right to rule Jammu by the Sikh ruler Ranjit Singh in 1820, and had conquered Kishtwar, Rajouri, and Ladakh through the 1820s and 1830s, began to harbour designs on the Kashmir Valley in the chaotic aftermath of Ranjit Singh's death in 1839. With his conquest of Baltistan in 1841, Gulab Singh controlled all the lands south and east of the Kashmir Valley, and thus the shawl-wool trade as well. From this position of strength, he inserted himself in the politics of the Punjab by offering his military services to the British against the Sikhs as well as his negotiating services once the British had secured a victory in 1846 (Bamzai 1962: 598–602).

These negotiations not only restored amity between the Sikh and British Indian governments, but more importantly, recognized Gulab Singh's sovereignty over territories made over to him by the colonial state. This was formalized in the Treaty of Amritsar on 16 March 1846, which transferred to Gulab Singh and his male heirs 'all the hilly and mountainous country with its dependencies situated to the eastward of the River Indus and westward of the River Ravi including Chamba and excluding Lahul', in exchange for a sum of 75 lakh rupees and an annual tribute (Aitchison 1983 [1929]: 21). The British hoped that this would contain the Sikhs and appease Gulab Singh's territorial ambitions, since he had a disciplined Dogra army at his command which posed a threat. This is also the reason that they helped the Dogra army defeat the recalcitrant Sikh governor of Kashmir so that Gulab Singh could take actual control of the Valley.

As we have seen, the Valley's politics had been linked to and influenced by Jammu and other surrounding hill states throughout its past; Kashmir's rulers often took shelter in these principalities during troubled times, and the principalities participated in dethroning and enthroning Kashmir's rulers, sometimes even entering into matrimonial relations with Kashmiri noble families. However, the princely state established an entirely new relationship between the Kashmir Valley and Jammu, creating a link between the two that has undergone multiple changes over the years, but survives to this day.

On the one hand, within the framework of the princely state, Kashmir was rendered subservient to Jammu, since the ruler hailed from the latter and derived most of his legitimacy from the region. At the same time, Srinagar, the capital and political and economic heart of the Kashmir Valley, was anointed the summer capital of the state, with the government residing there for six months each year, thus cementing the Valley's centrality to the Dogra polity. While important for a variety of reasons to the earlier Mughal, Afghan, and Sikh empires, for their rulers Kashmir was not much more than an outpost to be governed from afar. For the Dogras, on the other hand, it was a prized possession— the very zenith of their territorial ambitions—and a seat of their kingdom itself.

The self-fashioning of the Dogra dynasty thus proceeded in tandem with the appropriation of Kashmir into its discourse of legitimacy, which was itself articulated in the context of British colonialism. Alongside pacifying the frontier tribes, Khakas and Bombas in particular, and bringing commodity production and trade under the control of the state, Gulab Singh (r. 1846–57) set the stage for endowing the Dogra dynasty with a framework of legitimacy drawn from Hinduism, by reviving the law banning cow slaughter, construction of temples throughout the state, and the establishment of institutions such as the Dharmarth, which functioned as a trust, patronizing temples, charities, and schools (Bamzai 1962: 665; see also Rai 2004: ch. 1). Soon after his ascension to the throne, his son and successor, Ranbir Singh (r. 1857–85), consecrated a shrine to the worship of Lord Ram, from whom the dynasty, with the blessings of the colonial state, claimed descent.

These and other such policies, including the preparation of a descriptive survey of the ancient Hindu pilgrimage sites of Kashmir, followed by a comprehensive assessment of Hindu monuments by the archeological department of the state (Bamzai 1962: 790; see also Rai 2004: ch. 4), were designed to define the Kashmir Valley in terms of its Aryan, Sanskrit heritage and Hindu cultural and political past, of which the Dogras saw themselves as a continuation. Already firmly embedded in Jammu, the Dogra dynasty's source of legitimacy in Kashmir, on the other hand, rested on a tenuous link to a specifically religious (Hindu) past that excluded the majority of its population. As the Dogra state machinery became more elaborate, in part as a result of colonial intrusions, Kashmiris struggled to define their identities in this rapidly changing sociopolitical landscape, eventually focusing on Islam to delineate the community and its demands.

Administering Kashmir

The creation of the princely state had far-reaching implications for the political economy of Kashmir and the relationships within and between communities in the Valley. Certain trends, in particular the consolidation of social groups such as shawl merchants and Kashmiri Pandits, which had begun during late Afghan and

Sikh rule, were continued and strengthened until the late nineteenth century. By the end of the century, the colonial state's intensifying intervention into the state, the increasing influx of outsiders to run the ever-expanding state administration, and global trends such as the declining shawl trade meant an upending of social and economic relationships, a redefinition of links between rural and urban Kashmir, and the threat of obsolescence for particular social classes.[2]

The Dogra state's expanded state machinery reorganized and took control of agricultural production, revenue collection, as well as internal and external trade. While Kashmiri Pandits remained significant players within the revenue administration in particular, the state imported Punjabis and Dogras to run the administration, granting jagirs to them in return for service and loyalty to the state. This, coupled with the land settlement, replaced the older, mostly Kashmiri and Muslim, generation of *jagirdars* (land grantee), with a new, mostly non-Kashmiri and Hindu, landholding class. At the same time, shawl merchants, a powerful group that continued to thrive as the Dogra state took over the manufacture and trade in shawls through the institution of a Dagh Shawl department, came under severe economic pressure as the shawl trade declined in the 1870s in the wake of the Franco-Prussian war.[3]

The British desire to direct the political affairs of the strategically located Jammu and Kashmir grew with their increasing concern about Russian expansion in Central Asia in the late nineteenth century. This manifested itself in a rising tide of colonial criticism of the Dogra maharajas' inability to take care of their subjects and their unjust rule (see Gadru 1973), culminating in the land settlement in 1887, and the removal of Ranbir Singh's successor, Pratap Singh, from the throne in 1889, to be replaced by the British Residency and State Council to run the administration of the state.[4]

The land settlement, under the direction of the Residency, was ostensibly carried out to replenish revenue by curtailing the powers of 'unscrupulous' revenue collectors and converting a thriftless peasantry into a thriving community. This included, among other things, collecting revenue in cash and kind and fixing the state revenue demand in kind at a lower level, so as to allow the market rather than the state to determine grain prices (Lawrence 1996 [1895]: chs 7 and 8). Since the state had historically been responsible for supplying cheap grain to city dwellers, this immediately led to grain shortages in the city, hitting the poor, such as shawl weavers, already suffering as a result of the decline in the shawl trade, particularly hard.

As already mentioned, the settlement of jagir lands, along with state policies, replaced the long-standing

Kashmiri landholders with a non-Kashmiri group loyal to the state. As for the peasantry, although it did not become appreciably better off—since it continued to toil under a better-organized system of heavy taxation—the settlement did sedentarize this class and bring its plight into the limelight, rendering it into a significant focus of emergent political movements at the turn of the twentieth century and beyond (Zutshi 2004: 87–101).

More generally, improved communications with British India, with the opening of the Jhelum Valley Cart Road to wheeled traffic, led to increased trade with the Punjab. Silk supplanted shawls in the export economy of the Valley, and as its profitability grew, the state brought the silk industry, based in Srinagar, under its direct control. Increased export-oriented trade, along with the institution of large public works such as the construction of the cart road and the Gilgit road, and a steady growth in tourism to Kashmir led to an influx of money into the Valley. The 1901 census noted the general prosperity in Kashmir and an increase in prices to a considerable degree in the decade from 1891 to 1901, and by 1911, the population of Kashmir province, particularly urban areas such as Srinagar, had registered an increase as well, in large part due to rural–urban migration (Zutshi 2004: 101–4).

By the second decade of the twentieth century, cities such as Srinagar had begun to suffer from urban sprawl, congestion, and severe sanitation problems. Urbanization placed great pressure on grain stores, leading to grain crises throughout the late nineteenth and early twentieth centuries, which caused immense suffering among the urban poor. As people congregated in the city and its surrounding areas in search of work, the competition for jobs and demands for better working conditions intensified. The concentration of people adhering to differing religious ideologies in one place, as religious leaders moved to the city from outlying areas in the Valley and the Punjab in search of followers, aggravated conflict (Zutshi 2004: 105–17).

The princely state of Jammu and Kashmir was a unique entity, cobbled together through military campaigns and political agreements over the course of several decades.[5] Once consolidated by the 1880s, it included the two provinces of Jammu and Kashmir, with the Jammu province further subdivided into the jagirs of Poonch, Chenani, and Bhaderwah; and the frontier districts, known as the Wazarats of Ladakh and Gilgit. The fortunes of Kashmir were now intimately tied to the other entities within this state and the balance of power among them. The early Dogra rulers established an elaborate system based on the colonial bureaucracy to administer their newly acquired territories, creating separate civil, military, revenue and judicial departments, and importing outsiders to staff them. Much like the colonial state, moreover, while the Dogra state ostensibly maintained a policy of non-interference in the religious customs and traditions of its subjects, it drew its legitimacy largely from Hindu idioms and ideas, also defining Kashmir in Hindu terms. It was in the context of becoming a part of this new entity, with the state now ever-present in their lives, that the inhabitants of the Valley formulated and articulated their community, and religious and regional identities.

Defining Religion and Community

By the turn of the twentieth century, even ordinary people had experienced the momentous changes ushered in by the incorporation of Kashmir into the princely state. The socio-economic tumult resulting from the fact that this was the third imperial entity that Kashmir had become a part of in the past century made it seem to many that apocalypse was at hand. The state, although more interventionist, appeared more interested in patronizing the building of temples and religious schools than in redressing the plight of thousands of Kashmiri Muslims and their religious institutions. In the meantime, the Kashmiri Muslim gentry faced the loss of their socio-economic position along with their land, being replaced by largely non-Kashmiri Hindus. The only way that Kashmir's distinctive position as an especially blessed Islamic landscape could be maintained in this new scenario was by establishing the majority of its population as a community and drawing its contours around a particular definition of Islam.[6]

Not surprisingly, shrines, particularly urban ones, and shrine worship itself became the centre of these efforts at defining and articulating the Kashmiri Muslim community. We have already seen the significant position that shrines held in Kashmiri society; while their political power had diminished considerably over the course of the eighteenth and nineteenth centuries, their social and economic influence continued unabated. These institutions still had fairly large revenue-free land grants attached to them, over which the managers of the shrines exercised almost unlimited power. In addition, as centres of the Kashmiri textual, oral, and performative traditions, they helped define the ways in which people expressed their grievances and their religiosity, and their identification with their homeland and community. The religious figures associated with these institutions, collectively known as *pirzada*s—pirs, Sufi mystics, religious mendicants, petty ulema, mullahs, and so forth—were a powerful group with a firm foothold in rural and urban Kashmir who played a significant role in connecting the two by transferring goods and ideas between them.

Reasserting control over shrines, thus, was a particularly effective way for groups such as the landed elite, shawl merchants, and religious leaders, who were facing profound social and economic strains at this time due to the changes in Kashmir, to regain some of their waning influence. However, they faced resistance from emergent commercial social groups such as grain dealers and other petty traders eager to gain social recognition of their growing economic clout through association with religious institutions. Increasing pressures of urbanization in general, manifested for instance in grain shortages, formed the backdrop for the resultant contests over urban sacred spaces and determined their ideological vocabulary, which was geared towards defining Islam, the Kashmiri Muslim community, and ultimately also its leadership.

These conflicts over sacred spaces were most concentrated in the city of Srinagar, the sociopolitical and spiritual hub of the Kashmir Valley, and centreed on the issue of whether shrine worship was an acceptable Islamic practice and should continue to define Kashmiri Islam. The two head preachers, or Mirwaiz, of Srinagar, and their supporters and followers tussled throughout the late nineteenth and early twentieth centuries over their right to preaching at the city's main shrines and mosques. The Mirwaiz Kashmir had traditionally preached at the Jama Masjid and its surrounding localities, while the Mirwaiz Hamadani's sphere of influence included the Khanqah-i-Mualla shrine (Sayyid Ali Hamadani's shrine) and its surrounding areas. The troubles began when the Mirwaiz Kashmir attempted to increase his influence in areas beyond the Jama Masjid by preaching against shrine worship, labelling it sacrilegious to Islam. This precipitated an immediate response from the Mirwaiz Hamadani and his supporters, many of whom were not only shawl merchants and landed gentry, but also shrine administrators and managers; they could not countenance any threat to the source of their remaining social and economic influence in society—shrines and shrine worship. They argued, therefore, that for Muslims, shrine worship was the purest form of expressing devotion to Allah (Zutshi 2018a).

As the two Mirwaizes battled it out to anoint themselves the true leaders of the Kashmiri Muslim community, not just in the city but throughout the Valley, and the state became increasingly involved in dividing the city's sacred spaces amongst them, Kashmir's publications market was flooded with treatises, poems, pamphlets, and other writings on Islam and its practise in Kashmir. The religiosity of the poor, especially the peasantry, a class that had recently garnered attention as a result of the settlement, came under intense scrutiny, with one side asserting that they barely practised Islam under the influence of shrines and their pirs, while the other side countering that shrine worship was the only means through which the downtrodden could stay in touch with Islam.

The leadership of the Kashmiri Muslim community, and the community itself, remained divided throughout the first half of the twentieth century, with schisms manifesting themselves most often over the issue of shrine worship. The Mirwaiz of Jama Masjid, who officially opposed shrine worship, nevertheless sought control over Srinagar's major shrines as a means to secure and maintain his family's influence among Kashmiri Muslims. In addition, the Mirwaiz family claimed the leadership of the Kashmiri Muslim community through its support of religious and educational institutions. Since the state paid so little attention to education, the purpose of these institutions was to enliven the minds of benighted Kashmiri Muslims and unify them into a community under the banner of true Islam. The managers of the other shrines of Srinagar, such as Khanqah-i-Mualla, also established schools to promote their vision for the Kashmiri Muslim community (see Zutshi 2004: ch. 4).

Punjabi Muslim political and religious organizations became increasingly influential in determining the course of Kashmiri Muslim politics starting in the second decade of the twentieth century, and the community continued the struggle to define itself and present its case to the state. As the Ahl-i-Hadis, Ahmadiyya, and other groups took up the cause of Kashmiri Muslims to increase their own influence in the Punjab and British India in general, the contests for Kashmiri Muslim identities became entwined with Punjabi Muslim sectarian politics. The Dogra state emerged as the primary reference points for these struggles, not just for Kashmiri Muslims within the state, but also for Kashmiri Muslims and their Muslim supporters outside the state. In this context, a new, educated Kashmiri Muslim leadership took up cudgels on behalf of Kashmiri Muslims in the 1920s and beyond.[7]

Commemorating Kashmir

While debates about Islam, its definition, and how it should be practised had become a significant aspect of Kashmir's publications market by the turn of the twentieth century, thereby focusing attention on competing communitarian and sectarian identities, the idea of Kashmir as a sacred space that accommodated multiple religious and other affiliations endured in its self-confident narrative tradition. Textual, oral, and performance narratives in multiple languages—Sanskrit, Persian, Kashmiri, and Urdu—intermingled and built on the earlier tradition to enliven events and characters from Kashmir's past, thus allowing people to participate in the commemoration of their homeland while also providing a space for them to share the joys, sorrows, and trials of their everyday lives. It was not polemics about shrine worship and sectarianism that dominated these narratives, stories, and performances, but rather historical memories of characters such as Lal Ded, Nund Rishi, Sayyid Ali Hamadani, and Sultan Zain-ul-Abidin, whose lives embodied the very nature of Kashmir, the land, and provided examples of universal moral conduct in everyday life.

Much like in the eighteenth century and even earlier, mystics, storytellers, folk actors, minstrels, poets, and ordinary men and women participated in creating and consuming a historical memory of the land and its people. The regional vernacular, Kashmiri, which as we have seen had come into its own at the turn of the nineteenth century, by the turn of the twentieth formed a bridge between languages, genres, the elite and popular, and manuscript and print. Significant writers in Kashmiri from this period include Maqbool Shah Kraalwari (1820–1876), who wrote stinging poems about the lives of the peasantry and the atrocities of revenue collectors, and Wahab Pare (1846–1914), who not only translated Firdausi's *Shahnama* into Kashmiri, but also wrote the stridently anti-Dogra poem, *Darveshi* (c. 1880) (Zutshi 2004: 136–7).

Booksellers such as Ghulam Muhammad Noor Muhammad (GMNM), which had emerged in the context of the new market economy of Kashmir and its growing links with the Punjab while still maintaining connections to the old bazaar, played a vital role in disseminating Kashmiri compositions. By the 1920s, the bookshop was commissioning the publication of an assortment of Kashmiri narratives, which were then widely dispersed in cities and through the countryside by travelling salesmen and in fairs around shrines. When they took over the shop, the two brothers, Ghulam and Noor Muhammad, began hiring translators to render Persian classics into Kashmiri and patronized the composition of original Kashmiri tracts as well. The bookshop became a gathering place where these narratives were not just recited and purchased, but also spontaneously composed. A team of scribes permanently attached to the shop copied this poetry, which was eventually printed in short eight- to sixteen-page pamphlets (Zutshi 2014: 273–8).

Despite its waning status, especially with the replacement of Persian with Urdu as the state court language in 1889, Persian historical narratives continued to be produced and circulated throughout the late nineteenth and early twentieth centuries, many drawing freely from Kashmiri poetry and other writings. Although Persian narratives were certainly concerned with identifying the Muslims of Kashmir as a community within Kashmir's political and spiritual past, they were nevertheless steeped in the idea of Kashmir as a sacred space, even before the advent of Islam, and proudly defined it as home to a continuous tradition of historical and literary composition in Sanskrit and Persian. Kashmir emerged at the turn of the twentieth century as a fully formed idea, a geographical entity, and a Muslim-majority province within a princely state in British India, but with a distinct and continuous history and multilingual narrative tradition that yet set it apart from the multitude of other polities in the global sphere.

The upsurge in discussions regarding Kashmiri Muslim identities, which increasingly fell along a variety of sectarian lines in the context of Dogra rule, rapid socio-economic changes, and contacts with British India, did not, it is important to remember, overshadow the concurrent, and more unifying, discourse on the land of Kashmir. By this time, the idea of Kashmir as a sacred space and a mulk was firmly established within its narrative tradition, which continued to articulate these ideas within the transformed scenario of late nineteenth- and early twentieth-century Kashmir. Kashmir's narrative tradition self-confidently claimed Kashmir as the home of multiple groups of people who had played an equal role in defining it. Within this narrative public sphere, it was far more important to recount the heroic and sorrowful deeds of historical figures and the trials and tribulations of the masses rather than to focus on schisms and disagreements within Islam. At the same time, inclusivity within this tradition did not elide the increasingly significant idea that Kashmiri Muslims were marginalized within a Hindu princely state, an idea that would translate into political movements in the early twentieth century.

Notes

1. Kraalwari (1913: 3).
2. On the political economy of Kashmir, see Zutshi (2004: ch. 2).
3. By 1883, the shawl business had reduced by 50 per cent and by the 1890s the Dogra state had withdrawn from the industry and abolished the Dagh Shawl department.
4. Full powers were restored to Pratap Singh in 1923 and he ruled the state until 1925. He was succeeded to the throne by Hari Singh, who ruled until 1947.
5. For details, see Snedden (2015: 86–97).
6. On these debates, see Zutshi (2004: ch. 3).
7. See Chapter 5 of this book.

4

Orientalizing and Nationalizing Kashmir

The only Sanscrit composition yet discovered, to
which the title of History, can with any propriety be
applied, is the *Raja Tarangini*, a history of Cashmir.

—H.H. Wilson[1]

The orientalist H.H. Wilson's words, which began
his lengthy essay on the 'Hindu' history of Kashmir,
a loose, partial translation of Kalhana's *Rajatarangini*
published in 1825, established Kashmir's centrality
to the orientalist narrative of Indian history, literary
heritage, and culture. Unfurling over the course of the
nineteenth century, this orientalist project, focused as it
was on Kashmir's Sanskrit narratives, drew on them to
define Kashmir as the home of the original Aryans and

the font of Brahmanical Hinduism and later Buddhism. Furthermore, it reiterated Kashmir's exceptionality in the subcontinent as the birthplace of the only Sanskrit composition that was worthy of being labelled a history. By the time Wilson penned his essay, Kashmir had already achieved global fame as the source of one of the most beautiful and finest textiles in the world— the Kashmiri shawl. Eliding the institutional contexts for their production, European narratives linked the abilities of Kashmir's literati and artisans to produce fine literature and products to the inherent beauty of its landscape, thus further naturalizing Kashmir's uniqueness.

By the turn of the twentieth century, this narrative had been seized upon by the emergent discourse on Indian nationalism to articulate its own vision for the Indian nation and Kashmir's place within it. This chapter follows the idea of Kashmir as an ideal oriental—later (Indian) national—space in the interconnected local, imperial, national, and global contexts of the production, translation, and consumption of its literary and artisanal commodities. Much like the narrative traditions we have seen thus far that articulated particular ideas of Kashmir, the orientalizing and nationalizing traditions too were intermeshed with specific political and economic objectives.

Birthplace of (Indian) History

As with the subcontinent's Sanskrit tradition as a whole, European orientalists were introduced to Kashmir's Sanskrit narratives through Persian narratives from the Mughal period. Early in the nineteenth century, William Moorcroft—interestingly also an avid collector of Kashmiri shawls and researcher of their methods of production, as we shall see—followed by H.T. Colebrooke procured manuscript copies of the narrative, although it is unclear whether these were in Sanskrit or its Persian translations. These manuscripts, and some Persian histories of Kashmir, became the basis for H.H. Wilson's partial translation of *Rajatarangini*.

Wilson's essay had two objectives, both of which established the basis for the orientalist engagement with Kashmir through the rest of the century. First, the essay recognized Kashmir as the only region in the subcontinent that had produced a history and was home to an interconnected tradition of historical composition:

> The whole forming a remarkable proof of the attention bestowed by Cashmirian writers upon the history of their country, an attention the more extraordinary, from the contrast it affords, to the total want of historical enquiry in any other part of the extensive countries peopled by the Hindus. (Wilson 1825: 3)

From henceforward, *Rajatarangini* would come to stand in for the history of Kashmir, and following feverish searches for the original, authentic manuscript of the narrative, more orientalist ink would be spilled on translating and commenting on *Rajatarangini* than perhaps any other Sanskrit text.

Second, as the title of the essay, 'An Essay on the Hindu History of Kashmir', amply demonstrates, it instituted an enduring link between the history of Kashmir and the narrative of Indian history, particularly in its ancient, 'Hindu' period. For Wilson, what was important was not so much what *Rajatarangini* and its continuations revealed about Kashmir's history, but rather what they revealed about India's classical past before the Muslim invasions, a period, according to him, that was engulfed in darkness (Wilson 1825: 7, 82). For Wilson, thus, *Rajatarangini* was a history, and more importantly, a historical source par excellence, that established the chronology of Indian history; corroborated themes in early Indian history, such as the schism between Brahmans and Buddhists; and confirmed the emergent colonial, disciplinary periodization of Indian history into the Hindu, Muslim, and British periods (Wilson 1825: 83–5).

In some ways, Wilson was drawing on Abul Fazl's celebration of *Rajatarangini* and its continuations, which made Kashmir the centre of an interconnected tradition of historical composition, as well as on later Persian histories of Kashmir, which recognized *Rajatarangini* as the font of historical writing in Kashmir. However, for Wilson and the orientalists, and Indian nationalists who followed, Kashmir's historical tradition, as Kashmir itself, was to be harnessed to serve the needs of the larger Indian historical and nationalist projects.

Exceptional Region

By the late nineteenth century, the idea of Kashmir as the repository of India's classical, Aryan past was well-entrenched in orientalist circles. Within Kashmir itself, institutional practices put in place by the Dogra rulers further facilitated and disseminated the idea. Maharaja Ranbir Singh took concrete steps to establish the Hindu lineage of the Dogra dynasty and present Kashmir as the centre of Sanskrit civilization by, for instance, founding the Raghunath Temple and library, where Sanskrit manuscripts from Kashmir and all over India were collected and preserved. In addition, he patronized the production of new commentaries and digests in various branches of Sanskrit literature and the translation of several Sanskrit texts into Hindi (including *Rajatarangini*), as well as Persian and Arabic texts into Sanskrit through the establishment of a translation department.

The seamless alignment of the objectives of the Dogra and orientalist projects vis-à-vis Kashmir's literary history is particularly visible in M.A. Stein's activities in Kashmir, which began in the late 1880s. Registrar of Punjab University and Principal of Oriental College, Lahore, Stein prepared a critical edition of *Rajatarangini* (1892), followed by its translation into English (1900). His lengthy prefaces and introductions to both served to establish a link between Kashmir's ancient past and its present through the Sanskrit language (see Stein 1979 [1900], vol. 1: 1–144). Stein's interpretation of the narrative reinforced Kashmir's exceptionality, not just because it had produced a narrative that bore the characteristics of a history, but also because its past, according to Stein, followed a distinct, 'regional' trajectory.

Through his Kashmiri Pandit intermediaries, Stein drew heavily on Kashmir's oral and textual traditions as well as material sources to interpret *Rajatarangini*, endowing it with the status of a regional history. Moreover, based on his reading of Greek, Mughal, and Chinese sources, Stein accorded Kashmir with a distinctiveness and historical unity as a region since antiquity, noting, '*Nature itself* when creating the great valley of Kasmir and its enclosing wall of mountains, seems to have assured to this territory not only a distinct geographical character, but also a historical existence of marked individuality' (Stein 1979 [1900], vol. II: 386 [emphasis mine]).

Stein's edition and translation of Kalhana's *Rajatarangini*, thus, transformed the narrative into a synonym for Kashmir itself. From henceforward, Kashmir would be remembered through the generations into the present for its distinctiveness in producing the Sanskrit historical narrative par excellence, while the Persian tradition that followed it would be completely erased from memory. While its own narrative tradition had articulated Kashmir's exceptionality for centuries—and indeed Stein's writings on Kashmir echoed that tradition—Stein's work, and that of orientalists who preceded him, brought the idea of Kashmir as a special, distinct region to the attention of the rest of India and the world at large.

Kashmir and the Nation

The 'discovery' of *Rajatarangini* by European orientalists and colonial historians became especially significant for late nineteenth- and early twentieth-century Indian nationalists consumed with giving voice to the history of the nation. Since the colonial historical method had dismissed most other Indian, especially Sanskrit, narratives as biased and fantastical, *Rajatarangini*, with its aura of objectivity, became a critical source for this project. However, recognizing that it was a regional history, Indian translations of the text attempted to enfold it, and by extension Kashmir, into the emergent nationalist narrative in a number of ways. This section discusses two such English translations: a prose translation of Kalhana's text and its continuations by J.C. Dutt published in three volumes in 1879, 1887, and 1898, and a verse translation of Kalhana's text by R.S. Pandit published in 1935.

Dutt, a Bengali intellectual and brother of noted nationalist R.C. Dutt, translated the text with the express purpose of reclaiming India's past from colonial histories and from the myths and legends that it appeared to be steeped in. Much like Wilson, Dutt simply incorporated Kashmir's history into the Indian nationalist narrative, referring to Kalhana as 'the father of Indian history' (Dutt 1990 [1898], vol. III: i). According to Dutt, it was impossible to write the history of ancient India because the sources available for such an endeavour were replete with 'stories of the past mostly of an absurd and romantic kind' (Dutt 1879, vol. I: ii). The best that could be accomplished was to carry out a 'faithful rendering' into English of an already existent Sanskrit historical account of a people who lived in one corner of India (Dutt 1879, vol. I: iii). The Indian past thus brought to light was a purely Hindu one, uncorrupted by later Muslim interpolations. Moreover, deeply uncomfortable with the poetic flourishes and fabulous stories that so infuse Kalhana's narrative, Dutt simply edited them out of his translation to produce a dry factual narrative of Kashmir's history, which stood in for the history of ancient India.

Rajatarangini's translation held a somewhat different meaning for R.S. Pandit, Jawaharlal Nehru's brother-in-law, although for him, too, the narrative had to be read and interpreted as part of India's national heritage. Pandit was less interested in the narrative as a chronological record of past events as he was in it as an exemplary piece of historical literature—the Sanskrit *kavya*—that encapsulated Indian civilization's best moment and the character of its people. Thus, the insights put forward by Kalhana were not merely historical truths; rather, they were higher, more universal, moral truths (Pandit 1968 [1935]: xv). For Pandit, Kalhana did not consider history as an exercise in factuality but rather as a form of art that encapsulated the essence of life.

Pandit's translation elevated *Rajatarangini* to the status of a national text and a central part of the Indian literary canon. And yet, he did not altogether dismiss its historical value, since it gave voice to universal themes that defined the national narrative of Indian history. Moreover, Pandit utilized the text to shed positive light on the history of the nation by refuting colonialist claims about its past, including its autocratic forms of government, the inequities of the caste system, and the subordination of women by drawing a direct line between Kashmir's history as evident in *Rajatarangini* and the history of the putative Indian nation (Pandit 1968 [1935]: xxxii).

Pandit, thus, performed the double act of appropriating this history of a region into the nation's collective literary and historical heritage, while also incorporating the region into the nation. Nehru's foreword to the translation further affirmed the status of Kashmir as a crossroads of a variety of cultures that was nevertheless 'a part of India and the inheritor of Indo-Aryan traditions' (Nehru in Pandit 1968 [1935]: x).

Nationalist readings of *Rajatarangini* and by extension Kashmir were in many ways deeply indebted to earlier and concurrent orientalist, colonial readings of Kashmir's Sanskrit tradition. For both, Kashmir's history—and historical tradition—began and ended with *Rajatarangini*, before the advent of Islam, and along with it Persian, corrupted its landscape. Converging with the Dogra's state's political imperatives, Kashmir emerged in this discourse as the ideal Hindu historical space, simultaneously distinct from as well as a constituent part of larger Indian and nationalist historical and literary narratives.

Kashmiri Shawls in the Global Context

However significant Kashmir's Sanskrit narratives were to orientalists, the real reason for the spread of Kashmir's fame throughout Europe was not its narratives as much as its fine commodities. A product that Europeans seemed particularly enamoured with in the eighteenth and nineteenth centuries was the Kashmiri shawl, which became the material symbol of Kashmir to the Western world. The discourse surrounding its production, circulation, and consumption not only allows a glimpse into how Kashmir was defined and orientalized in a more global context, but also how Kashmiri shawls became the vehicle for ordinary Britons' engagement with empire.

The production and trade in Kashmiri shawls, as we have seen, had been a significant aspect of Kashmir's economy since at least the Mughal period. Lucrative as it was, it is no surprise that from its inception shawl production was a commercial, court-patronized, and state-controlled enterprise.[2] Since shawls were hand-woven from the fine hair—Pashmina—of the Central Asian mountain goat found in the Himalayan regions of Yarkhand, Khotan, Sinkiang, Lhasa, and Ladakh, the shawl wool trade to a large extent determined Kashmir's political relations with these regions. The manufacture of each Kashmiri shawl—from sorting the shawl wool to spinning it into yarn, from dyeing the yarn to weaving it according to specific patterns, and finally embroidering and washing the final product—was a labour-intensive process that involved women and men at various stages of production. The end product was, as a result, expensive. While the state and shawl merchants became wealthy on the sale of shawls, those involved in its production, particularly weavers and embroiderers, toiled away in near penury and miserable working conditions.

By the late sixteenth century, Kashmiri shawls were circulating as items of clothing and gift exchange far and wide, including in Mughal India, Persia, Russia, and the Ottoman lands, with distinct patterns, designs, and colours depending on the market (Maskiell 2002: 27–65). They made their way to Britain and Europe in the late eighteenth century as items of trade and as gifts for female relatives brought home by members of the English East India Company. Shawls had become so popular in Europe by the early nineteenth century that European merchants had their agents stationed in Srinagar to commission and directly purchase shawls to meet the demands of home markets. Furthermore, since Kashmiri shawls were beyond the reach of most middle-class consumers, an imitation shawl industry emerged in textile towns such as Paisley, Norwich, and Edinburgh, gaining ground at the turn of the nineteenth century as these towns competed with each other to produce a fine, durable, and inexpensive product that could rival the genuine shawl (Zutshi 2009: 423–4).

William Moorcroft's journals and other writings on shawl production formed an invaluable source of information for the British shawl industry. More significantly still, his descriptions of Kashmir's beauty, landscape, people, and products were endlessly reproduced in European writings on Kashmir through the course of the nineteenth century. As superintendent of the Company's stud farm, Moorcroft travelled extensively through British India, and in 1822–3 undertook an expedition through Kashmir, Ladakh, and Bukhara. While the stated purpose of this trip was to search for good horse breeds, Moorcroft's real objective was to collect information on the raw materials and production techniques used by the natives of these regions. He was especially interested in the possibilities of breaking into the shawl wool trade so that the British shawl industry could have access to this raw material, and in thoroughly understanding the processes involved in the manufacture of shawls (Alder 1985: 212, 297–8). After all, these techniques could not be allowed to remain in the hands of the ingenious, but oppressed and fraudulent, Kashmiri weavers; they had to be systematized into scientific knowledge that could be utilized more effectively by a modern, efficient industry.

These ideas about Kashmir, Kashmiri shawls, and the people who made them eventually filtered into the lively genre of writings on Kashmir, many by authors who had never themselves set foot in the region.[3] Such narratives performed two interrelated tasks:

First, they sought to educate Britons about the varied geography of the British Empire, in this case by focusing on one constituent part of it; and second, they translated the specialized knowledge about shawl manufacture transmitted by individuals such as Moorcroft by placing it within the larger discourses on imperial politics, industrialization, and consumption. Kashmir emerged in these narratives as an exceptional space on the fringes of empire, immaculate and stunningly picturesque, with its beauty invariably linked to the ability of its people—although 'wanting in civilization'—to produce delicate textiles such as the shawl (Anonymous 1875: 9–10).

The commodity and consumption culture of Victorian Britain, with its focus on the materiality and novelty of commodities, was critical to its engagement with the shawl, and by extension, Kashmir. What drove the intense desire for shawls, which became, as Vanessa Chishti has argued, 'a metonym for the Valley, embodying a quintessentially "Kashmiri" quality', was their perceived authenticity (Chishti 2018: 265). A Kashmiri shawl could be imitated, but the imitation shawls could never attain the fineness of the genuine Kashmiri shawl. This fineness was attainable only in the shawls made of the fine fleece available in Kashmir due to its geographical location, and woven by Kashmiris using primitive techniques while toiling away at their looms. Kashmir's extraordinary topography, its purer water, and its colourful flowers and birds spontaneously translated into the exquisite patterns and bright dyes of the shawls. These travel and other narratives, thus, dislodged shawl production from its economic and institutional contexts, reducing it to a pre-industrial endeavour set in the pre-capitalist paradise of Kashmir. The Kashmir shawl was valued precisely because it was considered a non-commodity (Chishti 2018: 266).

Moreover, the non-commodity and the place from whence it originated were deeply enmeshed with British colonial politics and hence also the imperial imagination. The very treaty that brought the princely state of Jammu and Kashmir into existence through the pact between the Dogra dynasty and the East India Company in 1846 ritually enacted the relationship through the annual gift of twelve shawl goats (six male and six female) and three pairs of shawls from the Dogra rulers to the British crown (Zutshi 2009: 424–5). A tract entitled *Kashmeer and Its Shawls*, anonymously published in 1875 on the occasion of the Prince of Wales' impending visit to Kashmir, took the opportunity to inform its readers about the British government's relationship with the princely state by celebrating its most well-known manufacture, which continued to serve as the material representation of the political and economic relationship between the two, endowing the former with suzerainty over its territories and the latter with political legitimacy to rule over them (Anonymous 1875: 12).

Not surprisingly, Ranbir Singh commissioned the production of a special shawl for presentation to the Prince of Wales on the same visit—a pale blue shawl that was minutely embroidered with the map of Srinagar (the centre of shawl production and the capital of Jammu and Kashmir). This was to serve as a recognition of the paramountcy of the British crown on the city of Srinagar and by extension the territories of the state, while at the same time claiming them as the Dogra ruler's sovereign territories. Kashmir was soon opened up to tourism as the British and Europeans flocked to it in the summer months to escape the searing heat of the plains and to hunt, swim, hike in, and otherwise partake of its much-famed natural bounty. Hitherto merely textual, the celebration of Kashmir's untouched splendour now took on a visual dimension with its landscape and products becoming one of the most photographed in the subcontinent (Kabir 2009: 93;

Zutshi 2009: 436–7). Thus, although not directly ruled by the British, Kashmir—through its manufactures and natural surroundings—became very much a part of the metropole's engagement with empire.

Within this engagement, while Kashmir's unspoiled beauty and the authenticity of its products had to be preserved, it also had to be subjected to the colonial-industrial order and modernity. These two strands competed with each other in late nineteenth-century representations of Kashmir, as the proponents of Britain's industrial might clashed with the votaries of movements such as the arts and crafts movement. For the former, which defended the production of cheaper shawl imitations as the sign of British industrial innovation, Kashmir was a beautiful, yet stagnant, place, where weavers continued to use ancient methods of production.

For the latter, shawl imitations were one of the many symbols of the ills of industrialization and commercialization, which were leading to the declension in taste and design. To remain sites of nostalgia for a more tasteful, innocent, pre-industrial past, Kashmir and its shawls could not be allowed to succumb to modern influences. This mystique, luxury, and sensuality surrounding Kashmiri shawls—as embodiments of Kashmir itself—generated by nineteenth-century European narratives, continues today to be associated with them not just in the West, but also in South Asia.

The images that we associate with Kashmir today—of a pristine, pure landscape, a somehow singular place, with its craftspeople producing objects of unparalleled fineness and beauty—were created through the course of the nineteenth century as Europeans came into contact with Kashmir and its literary and other products in the context of the British Empire.

Indian nationalists appropriated the resultant creation of the idea of Kashmir as a distinctive region to serve the interests of the nation. Kashmir was thus reduced to either certain Sanskrit texts, or its landscape, or its shawls, each decontextualized from its politics, economics, and institutions. Kashmir's multilingual, interconnected narrative tradition; its complex history; and indeed its inhabitants and their interactions with the world, received—and continue to receive—little space in earlier and current engagements with this region.

Notes

1. Wilson (1825: 1).
2. Until 1871, the government of Jammu and Kashmir derived annual revenues of Rs 600,000 from its taxation on shawls (Lawrence 1996 [1895]: 440).

3. Thomas Moore's *Lalla Rookh* (1817) was a significant example (see Chishti 2018: 268). The travelogues written by Godfrey Vigne, Victor Jacquemont, and Alexander Cunningham enjoyed wide circulation (see Alder 1985: 368).

5

Kashmir as Nation

I firmly believe that the freedom from the shackles
of an irresponsible Government is our birthright and
we should never rest until we get it.

—P.N. Bazaz to J. Nehru[1]

*Nahi shaya hai insaan ko zillat wa ghulami ki/ Ki jab
paida hua insaan hai azaad fitrat se* (Human beings are
not worthy of disgrace and enslavement/When they
are born with a free nature).

—'Meem', a liberal Muslim graduate[2]

The concept of freedom—from autocratic government,
humiliation, slavery, and exploitation—as expressed
here by Prem Nath Bazaz and 'Meem', was critical
to the emergent discourse on Kashmir as nation in
the early decades of the twentieth century. The ideas

of Kashmir as an exceptional sacred space, a mulk to be rescued from the depredations of outsiders, and an oriental region par excellence that we have discussed in earlier chapters, coalesced in this period in the definition of Kashmir as watan—a homeland of multiple communities in which everyone deserved to live and work freely.

At the same time, however, much like Indian nationalist discourse, the discourse on Kashmiri nationalism brought out—even as it simultaneously accommodated and elided—fissures along lines of class, region, and religious community that had become entrenched in Kashmiri society by the turn of the twentieth century. The resultant debates about how to define Kashmir, and which groups within it truly deserved a restoration of their rights and freedom, took place on the much larger canvas of similar debates in British India. Gathering force through the 1930s and 1940s, these contestations had frayed the Kashmiri nationalist project by the moment of Indian Independence and Partition, leading to Kashmir's own eventual partition along multiple lines soon thereafter.

Origins

The origins of Kashmiri nationalism have to be understood in the context of the politics of the

princely state of Jammu and Kashmir under Dogra
rule and its relationship with British India. As we have
seen in Chapter 3, the Dogra state, which legitimized
itself in Hindu terms, ushered in vast changes onto
Kashmir's sociopolitical and economic landscapes.
Most significantly, it gave rise to a Muslim leadership
willing to define Kashmiri Muslims as a community
and speak on the community's behalf to the state.
Although the project of defining the community was
a fraught one that bitterly divided Kashmiri Muslims
and resulted in battles over the control of sacred spaces,
the Muslim leadership championed their cause and
demanded a redressal of their grievances, especially in
the realm of education.

By the 1920s, the efforts of the state educational
department and the patronage of schools by the
Muslim leadership had created a class of educated
Muslims with aspirations to advance further, who
travelled to British India, particularly Lahore and
Aligarh, for higher education. The men came from
both affluent families of shawl traders and landed
gentry as well as less affluent families that had taken
advantage of educational advances.

British India opened up a new world for these
Kashmiri young men who came into contact with the
ideas propounded by an array of Indian literati and
leaders, including Muhammad Iqbal and M.K. Gandhi,

and had the opportunity to participate in the organizations and movements led by them. From their new vantage outside Kashmir, where they were also witness to the harsh treatment meted out to poor Kashmiri Muslims who travelled to these regions for employment as labourers, the students began to consider the situation within Kashmir with fresh eyes. Upon their return to Kashmir armed with degrees but poor prospects for employment, the young men became the cornerstone of the movement to demand economic and later political rights for Kashmiris. Organizations based in the Punjab, such as the All India Kashmir Committee, which had been at the forefront of illuminating the plight of Kashmiri Muslims under Dogra rule since the early twentieth century, and Muslim groups, such as the Ahmadiyyas, which saw in Kashmir the possibility of increasing their own sphere of influence, became their main supporters (Zutshi 2004: chs 4 and 5). From early on in its inception, then, the movement to uplift Kashmiris was closely influenced by politics, movements, and ideas in British India.

The groundwork for the movement, however, had been laid within Kashmir long before the young men returned from their sojourns in British India. Rural–urban migration, urban sprawl and congestion, poor working conditions in shawl, silk, and other factories, coupled with mounting unemployment and rising (and then falling) grain prices due to events such as the First World War and the economic depression, made Kashmir ripe for a revolt. Indeed, in 1924, silk factory workers struck work and organized protests for better working conditions, increase in wages, and an alleviation of exploitation by factory officials. The disturbances resulted in the arrest and deaths of several workers, and later the same year, the Muslim leadership presented a memorandum of demands to the viceroy of India, Lord Reading, on behalf of Kashmiri Muslims.

Although the state took swift action to crush these demands—which included the grant of proprietary rights to Muslim peasants whose land had been snatched from them, greater inclusion of Muslims in the state administration, abolition of forced labour, and the appointment of a European commission to consider the grievances of Muslims—they were instrumental in setting the stage for the later movement (Zutshi 2004: 197–204).

Jammu and Kashmir Muslim Conference and the Battle for Leadership

By 1932, with the help of the established Kashmiri Muslim leadership and Muslim organizations outside Kashmir, young men from the Kashmir Valley as well as Jammu, chief among them Sheikh Muhammad Abdullah, G.M. Sadiq, Bakshi Ghulam Muhammad, Muhammad Afzal Beg, Chaudhuri Ghulam Abbas, to name a few, had consolidated the movement into an organization called the All Jammu and Kashmir Muslim Conference. The primary objective of this organization was to increase the representation of Kashmiri Muslims in the state administration, not surprising given that its membership consisted primarily of unemployed, educated youth, bristling at their treatment at the hands of a state not particularly eager to change its policy of employing mainly non-Kashmiris and Hindus. In the early years of the movement, there was less concern for peasants, workers, and the exploited masses in general, since the focus remained on 'naukari [employment] politics', as pointed out by 'Meem' in his article in *The Hamdard* ('Meem' 1938: 55). Furthermore, since the movement had emerged to redress the absence of Muslims in particular in the state administration, it continued to define Kashmir as the homeland of the Kashmiri Muslim quom, as in the early twentieth century.

The movement began rather staidly in 1930 with a petition to the government against the new rules instituted by the Civil Service Recruitment Board that created hurdles for Muslim men in joining state administrative services. However, it gathered force in the next few years as the leadership demanded the community's rights through numerous memorials, speeches, and protests that sometimes descended into riots, attacks on homes and businesses, and firings on and killings of protestors in response. 'Islam in danger' became the rallying cry of this growing movement, as in the 1931 incident that is usually marked as its beginning, when the alleged insult of the Quran by a Hindu constable in Jammu Central Jail led to a series of incidents that culminated in the clash between a restive crowd and the police outside the Srinagar Central Jail on 13 July 1931, leading to the deaths of several protesters (Zutshi 2004: 211–14). Abdullah quickly made the return of Muslim shrines and mosques that were under state control to the Muslim community the main plank of the movement (Rai 2018b: 37–42).

Indeed, the battle for the control of the movement and the leadership of the Muslim community itself, which played out in the first few years of the 1930s between the established leadership of the Mirwaiz Kashmir and Abdullah and his followers, was carried out on the site of the Kashmir Valley's sacred spaces and the issue of shrine worship. Abdullah emerged as the leader of Kashmiri Muslims because he successfully outmaneuvered the Mirwaiz and his followers in the contest for the control of Srinagar's sacred spaces.

Much like in the earlier contests, he did this by presenting himself as the true representative of Kashmiri Islam and the champion of shrine worship, thereby drawing adherents not just from shrine managers, but also their substantial followings. His mellifluous recitations of the Quran, accompanied by incendiary speeches against the Dogra state from the pulpits of shrines and mosques across Srinagar, mesmerized Kashmiri Muslims, eventually displacing the Mirwaiz as representative of the community. By the mid-1930s, Abdullah could claim the mantle of sole political leader of the Kashmiri Muslims.

This leadership battle drew an enduring line of division between Abdullah's supporters, known as the *sher*s (lions, after Abdullah's title *Sher-i-Kashmir*), and the Mirwaiz's supporters, the *bakra*s (goats, after the beards worn by the Mirwaiz and his followers), which directed the course of Kashmir's politics at critical moments and continues to divide politics—as well as the city of Srinagar—in contemporary Kashmir. While the Mirwaiz accused Abdullah of being an Ahmadiyya and thus not a true Muslim, Abdullah levelled a much more serious charge against the Mirwaiz by calling him a puppet of the Dogra regime, thus presenting a stark contrast to himself as the rebel. These verbal battles hurled from the pulpits often descended into physical violence around shrines and in city lanes as it became divided into spheres of influence between the two groups (Bazaz 1934: 124–5).

It is also important to remember that Abdullah's focus on cultivating himself as the representative of Kashmiri Muslims laid the foundation for the divide between the Valley and Jammu, which would come to the fore with serious consequences later. Although Jammu Muslims joined hands with Kashmiri Muslims in the initial stages of the movement and even played a significant role in defining its course, their paths began to diverge as Abdullah grew increasingly popular in Kashmir and reluctant to share power with the Jammu Muslim leaders, such as Chaudhury Ghulam Abbas. Moreover, Abdullah attempted to separate himself and the Muslim Conference from Punjabi Muslim organizations and groups to assert his independence and to counter the accusations that he was a pawn of outside groups such as the Ahmadiyyas. Jammu Muslims and the leadership in particular, on the other hand, had always been oriented towards Punjabi Muslim politics and wanted to maintain close ties with Punjabi Muslim organizations.

The consolidation of Abdullah's position as paramount leader of Kashmiri Muslims was aided by the creation of a carefully constructed image of him as a man of the people, a pious Muslim who was at the same time secular. This was in the context of the growing realization that the peasantry and artisans were the true backbone of an anti-autocratic movement, and that it could not be successful without the support of the minority community of Kashmiri Pandits. Since many Pandits held positions in the state administration, and the movement had focused exclusively on increasing the Muslim share in these services, Pandits saw it as aimed specifically against their interests. Prem Nath Bazaz, Abdullah's friend and a Kashmiri Pandit leader who strongly believed in inclusive nationalism, presented Abdullah as a man who had risen from humble origins to take on the tyrannical state and alleviate the conditions of the poor and downtrodden regardless of religious affiliation (Bazaz 1934: 18, 63–4).

While Abdullah did come from fairly modest origins and grew up in straitened circumstances—his father, who passed away before his birth, ran a small shawl factory—Bakshi Ghulam Muhammad, who emerged as his deputy in these early years, belonged to a much poorer family. An able organizer with an ear to the street, Bakshi became critical to broadening the class basis of the movement to include the proletariat and the working classes by inducting them into the Muslim Conference and organizing them into labour associations. Furthermore, Abdullah's travels across the mofussil and the countryside to spread the message soon brought the suffering peasantry into its fold and widened the geographical influence of this hitherto largely urban movement based in Srinagar (Raina 1991, vol. I: 64–5, 174–6, 382–3). The time was now ripe for the movement to acquire a new name and orientation.

The Jammu and Kashmir National Conference and the Battle for Economic and Political Rights

The year 1939 is usually regarded as the turning point in the Kashmir movement because it was at this juncture that the Jammu and Kashmir Muslim Conference was converted to the Jammu and Kashmir National Conference. While this was indeed a significant moment in terms of nomenclature with the invocation of the terms 'nation', 'national', and 'nationalism', it was the culmination rather than the beginning of trends, as we have seen, that had been set in motion earlier in the decade. These trends, of uniting all classes and religious communities under the banner of the Kashmiri nation and working together for its freedom from exploitation and oppression, became the mantra of this movement, with Sheikh Abdullah as its sole leader. However, the divisions that had been sown earlier also made their reappearance in this period, as Abdullah's critics and opponents arrayed themselves against nationalism as the panacea for the ills plaguing Kashmiris.

As noted earlier, opening the movement to the working classes, peasants, and minorities was critical to its continued success at a time when it was under attack from opponents for being either too focused on Muslims (the government as well as Hindu groups inside and outside Kashmir) or not Muslim enough (older leadership of the Mirwaiz). Furthermore, the leadership's solidification of this trend has to be understood in the context of the increasing interest of the Indian National Congress in the princely states, especially Jammu and Kashmir, in this period. Kashmiri leaders such as Bazaz had drawn the attention of the Congress leadership to the Kashmir movement and its attempts to broaden itself, as evident in an exchange of letters between Bazaz and the president of the Congress, Jawaharlal Nehru, in 1936 (Bazaz—Gandhi—Nehru Correspondence 1936). The following year, Nehru had met Sheikh Abdullah and the two leaders seemed to have come to an understanding about the future direction of the movement.[3]

The conversion of the Muslim Conference to the National Conference was preceded by an intense public relations effort to recast the movement as one focused on the achievement of responsible government for all the subjects of the state. In a speech on 28 March 1938, Abdullah pointed out that Hindus and Sikhs too suffered under the same yoke of exploitation and irresponsible government as Muslims, and responsible government was possible only if all groups united against the common enemy: 'From henceforward we should avoid religious perspectives in our politics and present a joint effort towards the achievement of our prime objective.' He further reiterated the need to pay special attention to the condition of 'our peasants' and 'labor in the cities', organize them, and 'bring them under our flag'.

This speech was published in the 3 April 1938 issue of *The Hamdard*, a newspaper jointly founded and edited by Bazaz and Abdullah, which was dedicated to the dissemination of the new message of nationalism (*The Hamdard* 1938). The paper kept up a steady drumbeat of articles and poems in 1938–9 on the plight of the peasants and the pitiable state of Kashmiri villages, the need for a secular approach to politics, the importance of the inclusion of minorities, an understanding of poverty not through a religious but an economic lens, responsible government as an inclusive not majority government, and so on.

Kashmir the nation was central to this project and required a definition as well as a past. It was in this context that the movement invoked the exceptionality of Kashmir, rekindled its status as paradise on earth, and re-drew attention to the plight of the people of this mulk, bringing together the strands of the earlier narrative tradition to serve a new political purpose. Articles and poems celebrated Kashmir's beauty and uniqueness while lamenting its rule by outsiders, starting with the Mughals, and the havoc they wrecked on its landscape and people. Moreover, they highlighted the peaceful nature of Islam's advent and dissemination and the co-existence of religious communities in Kashmir's history.[4] While this nationalist discourse elided this point, the nation was synonymous with the Kashmir Valley. Abdullah, who had already claimed the mantle of Kashmir's Gandhi—as a deeply religious Muslim who nonetheless believed in accommodating religious minorities—became this nation's most fervent representative.

The nationalist project and its primary votaries came under almost immediate attack as they attempted to change the direction of the movement. The authors of a one-page proclamation published in summer 1937, for instance, appealed to Muslims to rise up against the movement because it was designed to wipe out any trace of Islam from Kashmir's politics under the guise of *wataniyat* and *quomiyat* (nationalism) (Basati 1937). Behind this defense of Islam and rejection of nationalism lay a deep fear of the marginalization of

Muslims' economic and political concerns and the eventual destruction of their majority in Kashmir.

Similar concerns over class and religious community, coupled with regional differences, motivated the split between the Jammu Muslim leadership and the National Conference, leading eventually to the former's reinstatement of the Muslim Conference in 1940–1. Although Jammu leaders such as Ghulam Abbas, Ahmad Yaar Khan, and Allahrakha Sagar initially supported the move towards an inclusive nationalism and even voted for the resolution that created the National Conference, they grew increasingly alarmed at the nationalist and secular rhetoric of the movement. Most Jammu Muslims who were part of the movement came from feudal backgrounds, and were thus less interested in alleviating the conditions of the poor and downtrodden than in protecting and representing the rights of Muslims against a Hindu administration.

Furthermore, they had strong ties with Muslim organizations from British India and had been active participants in their anti-*shuddhi* and other such campaigns.[5] They viewed the Congress with great suspicion and became uncomfortable as the National Conference leadership, particularly Abdullah, began to sound like a mouthpiece of the Congress Working Committee (Abbas 1950: 196–7). In the wake of the All India Muslim League's 1940 Lahore

Resolution, the divide between Jammu and Kashmir was institutionalized along the familiar lines of British India, with the Muslim Conference (based largely in Jammu) allying itself with the Muslim League, and the National Conference (based largely in Kashmir) with the Congress (Zutshi 2004: 261–7).

By late 1940, thus, the Kashmiri nationalist movement found itself in a tight spot. Several significant Muslim members had deserted the National Conference in the wake of the Lahore Resolution; the Mirwaiz had found a new lease on life after joining the Muslim Conference and becoming its leader in Kashmir in 1941; the Maharaja's government had turned prominent Kashmiri Pandits against the organization, and its local Muslim supporters were busy capitalizing on the war effort and thus in no mood for a confrontation with the regime (Raina 1991, vol. I: 168–9, 207). The leadership had to find a way to maintain Kashmiris' interest in the movement and re-energize the masses, for which they turned to producing a radical policy platform that would give voice to its objectives.

The influence that communists had come to exercise on the Kashmiri nationalist movement by the 1940s is plainly evident in the resultant document. As Andrew Whitehead has illustrated, communists had been active in Kashmir politics since the late 1930s and by the 1940s had drawn many Kashmiri leaders into their fold (Whitehead 2015: 134–5). Although the *Naya* [New] *Kashmir* manifesto was the brainchild of these non-Kashmiri and Kashmiri individuals, including B.P.L. Bedi and Freda Bedi, and bears the imprint of communist ideology, the earlier Kashmiri Muslim leadership had envisioned, even demanded, as we have seen, many of its provisions.

Released in pamphlet form, with an image of a woman unfurling the National Conference flag (white plough on a red background), the manifesto was adopted in the 1944 session of the National Conference and presented in person to the Maharaja. In its introduction, Abdullah defined the watan's struggle as a *jihad* (battle) of the poor against their powerful exploiters, and freedom from economic expropriation as the basis of political freedom and democracy. Furthermore, he reiterated the close link between the Kashmiri and Indian nationalist struggles during time of war, while also celebrating the victory of Russia over Germany as evidence of the power of economic freedom (Abdullah in *Naya Kashmir* 1944: 11–12). The text of the document advocated freedom of speech, press, and assembly as well as equal rights irrespective of race, religion, nationality, birth, or gender. It also provided for universal suffrage for those aged 18 and over to participate in the election of a national assembly that would exist as part of a constitutional monarchy subject to the authority of the Maharaja (Whitehead 2015: 316).

Meant less as an implementable policy programme and more as a rhetorical device, the *Naya Kashmir* manifesto did, to an extent, energize the masses. Abdullah appeared to be living up to his image as a saviour of the exploited and oppressed people of Kashmir. However, the manifesto's revolutionary message did not particularly speak to the more affluent sections among Kashmiri Muslims, some of whom had benefited from the reforms set in motion by the Dogra state on the recommendations of the Glancy Commission—which had been established to redress Muslim grievances after the 1931 disturbances—and did not identify with the struggle for the rights of the subjugated masses. More significantly, within the organization itself, those who resented the overweening influence of communists began to air their feelings, leading to a cleavage between the pro- and anti-communist factions of the party (Raina 1991, vol. I: 213–14).

Abdullah attempted to stay above these growing divides, not wanting to alienate educated Muslims who might be susceptible to the Muslim League's message, or the communists, or those who were against them (including the Congress). He did recognize, however, that the organization was fraying, which became even more apparent as the relationship between the National Conference and the Dogra regime, under the prime ministership of R.C. Kak since 1945, deteriorated rapidly. The leadership did not know how to respond to Kak's tough tone against their demands and by 1946 appeared paralyzed; the imperative of taking the movement in a new direction became increasingly evident to Abdullah. The deliberations of the Cabinet Mission on the constitutional future of India provided the opportunity to do just that.

Quit Kashmir, the Poonch Uprising, and Division

A movement that had not long before pledged to uphold a constitutional monarchy in the *Naya Kashmir* manifesto now issued a memorandum to the Cabinet Mission demanding—given the impending lapse of British paramountcy over the princely states—the abrogation of the Treaty of Amritsar, the end of the Dogra dynasty's rule over Jammu and Kashmir, and the transfer of sovereignty to the people of Kashmir. Authored by Abdullah, 'Quit Kashmir: Memorandum to the British Cabinet Mission', took the opportunity to reassert the Valley as not only 'our homeland', but also as the 'cradle of the Kashmiri nation, which by virtue of the homogeneity of its language, culture and tradition and its common history of suffering is today one of the rare places in India where all communities are backing up a united national demand' (Abdullah 1946: 2). It concluded with an appeal to the Cabinet Mission to end the princely order and settle the 'fate of the Kashmiri nation' (Abdullah 1946: 16).

Quit Kashmir caught the party leadership within Kashmir by complete surprise. The party lacked the organization, funding, and support necessary to carry out a movement of this kind, especially at short notice. Some within the party felt that it was the communists that had put Abdullah up to this 'mad adventure' (Raina 1991, vol. I: 267–8, 293). In the meantime, the regime's response was swift, as the state army took over Kashmir overnight, and began arresting key figures, starting with Abdullah, thus placing most of the National Conference leadership behind bars by the autumn of 1946. The movement went underground, supported by the communist network and run by Kashmiri leader G.M. Karra, who had evaded arrest, as well as Kashmiri women, including Mahmooda Ali Shah and Begum Zainab. Some leaders, such as Sadiq and Bakshi, managed to cross over into the Punjab to provide logistical assistance from outside and drum up support for the movement in India (Whitehead 2015: 138–9).

From the perspective of the Congress leadership, Quit Kashmir put them in the uncomfortable position between supporting a movement that was aligned with their goals, and a princely ruler, whom they did not want to alienate. Many leaders, such as Sardar Vallabhai Patel and J.B. Kripalani, viewed the movement with suspicion because it challenged the right of the princes to decide on their states' future and was being directed by communists. Thus, even the more sympathetic among the leaders, such as Nehru, focused on denouncing the acts of repression and violence against the people that were being perpetuated by the Dogra regime, rather than on the abrogation of the treaty and the right of Maharaja Hari Singh to rule Kashmir (Raina 1991, vol. I: 335–6, 338–41).

The movement likewise placed the Muslim League in a dilemma because it too was caught between two poles—on the one hand, the Muslim Press in the Punjab, which stridently supported the movement, presenting Abdullah as a hero while painting the Maharaja as a villain, and on the other hand, its own policy of supporting not just princely rulers, but also the rival of the National Conference—the Muslim Conference—in Kashmir. Muhammad Ali Jinnah, the president of the Muslim League, asked the Muslim Conference not to overtly support the movement and to contest the assembly elections that had been called by the Maharaja for early 1947. This in turn placed the organization in an impossible position and divided its leadership, with the Mirwaiz Kashmir loudly denouncing the movement as anti–Islamic, while Ghulam Abbas attempted to toe a middle line because although he was bound to follow the Muslim League's instructions, Jammu Muslims, whom he represented, were vehemently anti-Maharaja. Soon, therefore, Abbas made a fiery anti-Maharaja speech and was arrested, removing him from active Jammu politics by October 1946 (Saraf 1977, vol. I: 689–95; Raina 1991, vol. I: 343).

By late 1946 and early 1947, National Conference leaders were deeply despondent about the state of the movement. Not only had the two main political parties of British India offered at best some support for the movement and at worst condemned it, interest in it seemed to be flagging even among the National Conference's loyal supporters within Kashmir itself. The Kashmiri nation and its tribulations seemed to be far from the minds of the people of the 'cradle of the Kashmiri nation', spent as they were in the face of relentless repression and economic distress. To add to its woes, *The Hamdard*, still edited by Bazaz—who had parted ways with Abdullah by the early 1940s—kept up a barrage of articles against the movement, describing it as a ploy cooked up by Abdullah to revive a languishing organization.[6] Thus, Quit Kashmir failed to achieve much in concrete terms and in some ways even backfired on Abdullah. Perhaps most importantly, since the Maharaja refused to release Abdullah and the rest of the leadership from prison, they were absent from the political scene at the most crucial moment of the subcontinent's, indeed also Kashmir's, history.

Abdullah was finally released in late September 1947 after continuous pressure by the Congress leadership on the Maharaja. He had to pledge loyalty to the ruler, thereby at least temporarily giving up on the objective of Quit Kashmir. By this time, India and Pakistan had come into existence as independent states, and Jammu and Kashmir was sovereign, since British paramountcy had lapsed and the Maharaja was dithering on whether to join India or Pakistan— which was his choice as provided for by the terms of the Cabinet Mission plan—or to continue to exist as an independent entity that had relations with both. Abdullah attempted to sidestep the question by demanding 'freedom before accession'—or freedom from the irresponsible Dogra government—and time to consider Kashmir's options before making a decision about Kashmir's future status in the subcontinent. Back-room diplomacy was in full swing at this time as National Conference leaders negotiated with the Pakistani and Indian leadership on the terms of a possible accession (Zutshi 2004: 307–8).

However, several events were already in motion that snatched the political initiative from the hands of the National Conference before any decision could be arrived at. These were the culmination, at least in part, of the focus of the National Conference—and the Congress—on the Kashmir Valley as the centre of the Kashmiri nation to the exclusion of other parts of the state. As Abdullah went around making speeches in late September and early October, he did not in any way acknowledge the presence of the Muslim Conference, which although in disarray since Abbas continued to languish in prison, had its own ideas about the future of the state. Not only did the members of the party, some in the Valley and most in Jammu, not recognize Abdullah as their leader or his definition of nationalism, most felt that their interests would be best served through the state's accession to Pakistan.[7]

More significantly, Muslims of western Jammu province, in particular the jagir of Poonch, were especially anti-Dogra and pro-Pakistan for a variety of historical and other reasons. This region had deep interconnections with the economies, people, and movements of the Punjab and the North West Frontier Province (NWFP). Moreover, Poonchis had been living under a system of dual oppression with the Dogra state as the suzerain and the Raja of Poonch as his vassal, and thus subject to an exploitative feudal regime that imposed heavy taxes while simply ignoring the reforms implemented in other parts of the state in the wake of the 1931 Glancy Commission recommendations. Limited economic opportunities had driven many Poonchi (and Mirpuri) men to join the British Indian army during the World Wars; in 1947 these several thousand demobilized men significantly outnumbered the Dogra army (Snedden 2012: 27–32). The National Conference had attempted to make inroads in Poonch—the fifth annual session of the organization in 1937 under the leadership of Abdullah was held there—with limited success (Zutshi 2004: 251).

As Christopher Snedden argues in his writings, it is important for us to shift our focus from Kashmir to Jammu if we are to understand the genesis of the Kashmir dispute in 1947. He notes that it was the Poonch uprising against the Maharaja—which began in August 1947 and had become an organized revolt by September—that instigated the future division of the state. As Jammu descended into inter-religious violence, and the Dogra army began to perpetuate atrocities against Poonchi Muslims, the simmering discontent against Dogra rule erupted into full-scale revolt. Under the leadership of individuals such as Sardar Ibrahim Khan, a relatively lesser-known member of the Muslim Conference from Poonch, Poonchi Muslims were organized into an army whose primary objective was to free the state from Dogra rule and merge it with contiguous Pakistan. While Abdullah was demanding 'freedom before accession' in Srinagar, the real action was taking place in Western Jammu, where the Azad Army, as it was called, had already freed large parts of Mirpur and Poonch from Dogra rule by the time the Pukhtoon tribesmen joined the fight on 22 October 1947. And two days later, it declared the formation of the Provisional Azad Government (Khan 1965: 69–80; Snedden 2012: 39–45).

Thus, it was this insurrection against Dogra rule rather than the incursion of the Pukhtoon tribesmen that set the stage for the division of the state. The incursion did encourage the Azad movement to imagine the possibility of bringing the Kashmir Valley within its purview. However, the tribal army, consisting of a loose band of fighters from the tribal areas bordering Afghanistan, who had entered the state to help their Muslim brethren and ensure that the state acceded to Pakistan, was also interested in booty. Their looting, raping, pillaging, and murdering in Baramulla in particular not only delayed their advance to Srinagar (see Whitehead 2007), but also helped Abdullah and India to tarnish any opposition to Abdullah's regime, which included the Azad government, by labelling them as a marauding external force supported by Pakistan.

Most importantly, it allowed time for the Maharaja to seek Indian military help, and led to his agreement to the state's accession to India on 26 October. In his acceptance letter, Lord Louis Mountbatten, India's governor general, noted that since the accession had taken place in 'special circumstances', 'as soon as law and order have been restored in Kashmir and her soil cleared of the invader, the question of the State's accession should be settled by a reference to the people'.[8] Indian forces were flown into Srinagar airport on 27 October to successfully prevent the Valley from falling into the hands of the opposing army. Further, the Maharaja's accession to India prompted another part of the state—Gilgit—to revolt against the Maharaja's authority on 1 November 1947, and declare for accession to Pakistan, which has yet to fully accept this accession (Sökefeld 2018: 135–6).

The locus of events now shifted to Srinagar with the Maharaja's appointment of Abdullah as the head of the emergency administration and his own hasty departure from the state. The National Conference seized this opportunity to consolidate its authority and form a People's Militia, and from its base at the city's Palladium Cinema, the party eventually took control of the entire administrative apparatus. Young Kashmiri men and women rushed to join the militia to defend their capital from the approaching army, while Abdullah made speeches exhorting the population to maintain communal harmony and protect the minorities. Communist influence was highly visible in the militia as well as the new Abdullah administration, as communist leaders and functionaries founded a Cultural Front to fashion a narrative of secular harmony—*Kashmiriyat*—that represented the Kashmiri nation and its new government (Whitehead 2015: 142–6). Communist presence in Kashmir would become a matter of great concern to the Government of India in the following months and years (Raina 1991, vol. II: 437).

In the meantime, as Indian forces battled Pakistani and Azad forces, an equally intense publicity war between India and Pakistan reduced the former princely state into a disputed territory between the two states, thus denying the people of the constituent parts of the state any say in its future status. This was exacerbated by India's internationalization of the issue, when it took Pakistan's actions to the United Nations (UN) on 1 January 1948 (Snedden 2012: 77–9).[9] Both states conveniently labelled any attempt to question their particular stand on the issue as fomented by the other side and not a genuine expression of political grievances by the state's inhabitants. For India, thus, the Azad movement was simply a front for Pakistan, while for Pakistan, Abdullah and the National Conference were merely Indian puppets.

Although the state of Jammu and Kashmir was not part of the partition plan that brought India and Pakistan into existence, the actions of the two countries had successfully partitioned it into the Indian state of Jammu and Kashmir; Pakistani Azad Kashmir; and the Northern Areas of Pakistan (now Gilgit–Baltistan) by 1949, a partition that is yet to be recognized by either country. The de facto border between the two states, known as the Ceasefire Line (now the Line of Control, LOC), was drawn where the Indian and Pakistani troops laid down their arms on 1 January 1949. Although not a de jure border with a specific past, the LOC has nevertheless become 'ideologically sacrosanct', creating its own history of violence and aggressive militarization in the region (Banerjee 2010: 62–3; see also Leake and Haines 2017).

The Jammu–Kashmir Valley divide, in place since the late 1930s, was to prove critical to the way the accession drama played out, with parts of Jammu going their own way against the Maharaja and towards Pakistan *before* the official accession to India, while the Valley, under threat from the tribal incursion, came into India's fold after the accession. Indeed, this divide would prove critical even after the partition of the state into its Indian and Pakistani parts, in particular in the Indian state of Jammu and Kashmir, and continues to do so into the present. The de facto partition ensured that

Kashmir was reduced to a regional territorial dispute between India and Pakistan—both of whom claimed the state in its entirety—with international implications, rather than what it actually is, as Martin Sökefeld puts it, 'an intricate entanglement of antagonistic political aspirations and relations of belonging, of power and resistance, of boundaries drawn and movements pushed forward or restrained that make up the "fragmented whole"' (Sökefeld 2018: 133).

Notes

1. Bazaz–Gandhi–Nehru correspondence, *The Hamdard* (1936: 4).
2. 'Meem', *The Hamdard* (1938: 55).
3. This was a time when the Congress was concerned with its failure to attract Muslims into its fold and had begun a Muslim mass contact programme in response. Jammu and Kashmir held some promise in this regard as a Muslim-majority state.
4. See *The Hamdard*, 31 July 1938, 'Responsible Government Number'. The first National Conference regime (1948–53) would institutionalize this idea as *Kashmiriyat*.
5. Anti-shuddhi campaigns attempted to counter shuddhi (purification) movements led by organizations such as the Arya Samaj that focused on the re-conversion of Muslim converts back to Hinduism.
6. See articles in *The Hamdard* (May 1947).

7. When a small faction within the party passed a resolution for the state's independence under the aegis of the Maharaja in July 1947, a larger faction hastily passed a counter-resolution for the state's accession to Pakistan (see Saraf 1979, vol. II: 709–13).

8. For these documents, see Das (1971, vol. I: 339–43).

9. For the text of India's complaint, see Das (1971, vol. I: 345–50). See also Chapter 6 of this book for further discussion.

6

Fragmented Kashmir

> The relationship that we entered into with India is
> neither one of complete merger nor one of
> complete independence.
>
> —Sheikh Muhammad Abdullah, July 1953[1]

This statement encapsulates the ambivalence of the
political relationships that emerged in the aftermath of
1947 between the constituent parts of the erstwhile
princely state of Jammu and Kashmir and the
newly emergent South Asian states that they were
incorporated into. In an era of indivisible sovereignties,
the fraught nature of these relationships—between
India and the state of Jammu and Kashmir; Pakistan
and Azad Kashmir; and Pakistan and Gilgit-Baltistan—
has been elided by the two states. Instead, as in the
case of Sheikh Abdullah, anyone who drew attention

to their existence was summarily dismissed, only to be replaced by individuals and parties more committed to unitary loyalty to an indivisible sovereignty. This chapter argues that the story of Kashmir in the post-1947 era is precisely a story of divided sovereignties, artificial borders, and actual and political movements that separate even as they bring together disparate entities under the rubric of the Kashmir dispute, thus rendering the region into a 'fragmented whole' (Sökefeld 2015a: 253).

Rather than examining this period from the perspective of the Indo-Pakistan conflict over the erstwhile princely state, with each claiming it in its entirety,[2] the chapter examines the internal politics of the constituent parts and their interactions and negotiations with, as well as resistance to and affirmation of, the Kashmir dispute over the course of the past 70 years. This allows us a glimpse into the failures of nation- and state-building on South Asia's margins, while also illustrating the complexities of the dispute and its intractability, since it involves more than simply India, Pakistan, and the Kashmir Valley. As we have seen, in part, it was the inability of the Kashmiri nationalist movement to effectively move beyond the Kashmir Valley to include the aspirations and demands of the multiple sub-regions of Kashmir within its ambit that resulted in the division of the state into several entities with tenuous relationships to India and Pakistan.

We cannot, as scholars, reproduce the blind spots of the Kashmiri nationalist movement and the nation-states by ignoring the multiple boundaries that cut across this region, creating a situation of ongoing partition for its inhabitants (Zutshi 2015). These divides exist not just among entities such as Azad Kashmir, Gilgit-Baltistan, and Indian Jammu and Kashmir, but also within these entities, and in their relationships with India and Pakistan. It is this 'shared political predicament' of having distinct political trajectories that are at the same time tied to the broader Kashmir question that has subjected the constituent parts of Kashmir to new forms of colonization in the period since 1947 (Sökefeld 2005; Sökefeld 2015a; 260).

Indian Jammu and Kashmir, 1947–53

Although Jammu and Kashmir was officially divided as a result of the drawing of the Ceasefire Line on 1 January 1949, the myth of its unity remained intact until well after this moment. The National Conference regime, which took control of the emergency administration and subsequently over the governance of what came to be called the Indian state of Jammu and Kashmir, claimed to speak on behalf of the entire population of the state. In the process, it revived and refashioned the idea of Kashmir as a paradise on earth to fit within the secular, nationalist narrative of the Indian nation-state. Within these mutually reinforcing narratives, Kashmiris had willingly chosen to be a part of India and Indians had accepted Kashmir into the Indian fold, because both sides were committed to economic and political reform within a secular framework. Furthermore, Kashmiri–Indian cooperation had thwarted Pakistan's attempt at forcefully taking over Kashmir based on its Muslim majority by sending in tribal raiders, and it was only a matter of time before the Indian army would reclaim all the territories of the state that were being illegally occupied by Pakistan.

Not only did Pakistan and Azad Kashmir challenge these narratives, but even within the Kashmir Valley and India not everyone subscribed to these ideas, especially as the first and then subsequent regimes in Jammu and Kashmir failed to live up to the ideals of instituting a new Kashmir free of economic and political privation. This was compounded by the steadily rising divisions within the state as a whole, as Jammu in particular began to assert itself against the domination of the Kashmir Valley and its leadership. Further complicating matters was the internationalization of the issue, which achieved little else beyond bringing Indian and Pakistani troops to a ceasefire while their governments continued to battle out their competing territorial claims.

This put enormous pressure on successive Jammu and Kashmir regimes to prove their loyalty to India at the expense of their citizens' rights. Over the decades, thus, India came to support, maintain, and manage autocratic regimes in Jammu and Kashmir, which were not answerable to the people. As corruption and nepotism soared, so did Kashmiris' discontent with government—both Indian and their own. The project of Kashmiri nationalism as envisioned by the National Conference in 1939, followed by 1944, had failed, not because it was incompatible with Indian nationalism, but because it hewed too closely to it.

The first Jammu and Kashmir regime headed by Abdullah as prime minister took power at a time of intense turmoil, both in the state and the subcontinent as a whole. Several parts of the state were in the process of breaking away and declaring their allegiance to Pakistan, a war between India and Pakistan was raging in large parts of it, and the rest of it was overrun by refugees flooding in from the Punjab to escape Partition violence. There was large-scale inter-religious violence within the state itself, particularly in the Jammu province. The raiders had almost made it to the gates of the capital, Srinagar, and the Maharaja's government had collapsed. The state almost immediately faced an intense economic crisis with acute shortages of essential commodities, including food grains and salt. India could do little to help in this regard because it was itself suffering from a severe depletion of food supplies. While Kashmiris had united in the face of the onslaught of the raiders, once the war showed no signs of an early resolution and the economic crisis continued, the fissures within began to come to the fore, including within the National Conference itself.

Given this context, it would have been difficult for any government to assume, consolidate, and maintain power, and Abdullah's regime was no exception. Its response was to either marginalize critics, including communists, or to coopt them by handing out favours, as in the case of union leaders, effectively rendering its own power bases ineffectual. The more vocal critics, especially those who questioned the state's accession to India and expressed an affinity for Pakistan, were either imprisoned, deported to the other side, or went into voluntary exile to Azad Kashmir. As disillusionment deepened among ordinary people, the regime introduced wide-ranging land reforms as a means to salvage its reputation. The land reforms, which included the abolition of large landed estates without compensation and the redistribution of land to peasants, provided further opportunities for corruption (Korbel 1954: 284–5; Tremblay 2018: 226–7). More significantly, the reforms alienated a substantial section of Jammu Hindus whose lands were resumed under the reforms and who were already smarting at the decline of the Maharaja's authority.

Caught in an impossible situation as prime minister, and facing mounting criticism on all fronts, Abdullah careened between multiple mutually exclusive positions in an attempt to placate all sides. As his primary constituency, Muslims of the Kashmir Valley, grew increasingly discontented at the lack of resolution of the dispute and a denial of their right to free expression, Abdullah resorted to attacking the Maharaja and demanding an end to his rule. While declaring his loyalty to India and his commitment to secularism, he also insisted on Kashmir's right to its autonomy and focused on increasing Muslim representation in state services and the army.

Rather than addressing the concerns of Jammu Hindus, he responded to their criticisms by labelling them communalists who were under the influence of Indian Hindu right-wing organizations and, therefore, could not abide the idea of being ruled by a Muslim regime. This only increased the influence of such organizations in Jammu, which supported the Jammu Praja Parishad's movement against Abdullah's regime that had gathered force by mid-1951, demanding complete integration of the state with India. This received a further fillip after the elections to the state constituent assembly in September 1951, all 75 seats in which were won by the National Conference through what were seen as a variety of nefarious means (Korbel 1954: 287–8).

At the global level, Abdullah insisted on the legitimacy of India's claim to Kashmir, especially at the United Nations. At the same time, he gave interviews to foreign correspondents in which he stated that Kashmir might be better off not being connected to either India or Pakistan, but maintaining friendly relations with both.[3] Throughout his tenure as prime minister, Abdullah incessantly went back and forth on the issue of Kashmir's accession to India, in a simultaneous attempt to not alienate either India or his base in the Valley. For instance, on the same day in Delhi in February 1948, he gave two speeches, in one stating that the accession to India had the will of the Kashmiri people behind it and in the next declaring that 'Kashmir will accept nothing less than independence'.[4]

India remained committed to the idea that once peace had been restored, the status of Kashmir would be settled with reference to the will of the people. It took Pakistan's actions to the UN under Article 35 of the UN charter, alleging that Pakistan had attacked its sovereign territory by sending tribal raiders into

Jammu and Kashmir. Pakistan's response was to accuse India of perfidy and force in acquiring the accession of the state. The UN, thus, came to adjudicate this dispute rather than India's original compliant, and passed several resolutions that called for a plebiscite in the state to determine the will of the people. India supported plebiscite in principle as long as the state was cleared of Pakistani troops, including the Azad Army, and a neutral plebiscite administrator was appointed.[5] Abdullah himself, interestingly, was against plebiscite, because he regarded it as questioning his authority to represent the views of all Kashmiris.[6] India's prime minister, Jawaharlal Nehru, was convinced that Abdullah was critical to ensuring India's victory in a future plebiscite because he was the most popular leader in Kashmir and, therefore, supported Abdullah and his regime despite their obvious failings and challenges to Indian authority.

These challenges were most apparent in the negotiations regarding the status of the state within the Indian constitution. At the time of Independence, all former princely states had acceded to the Indian Union only in three subjects—Foreign Affairs, Communication, and Defence—and had to be brought under Indian constitutional purview in all subjects. The case of Jammu and Kashmir was a bit different because since it was a disputed territory and its status was under adjudication at the UN, it could not be integrated beyond the three subjects; however, its relationship with India had to be more precisely spelled out in the Indian constitution. Abdullah pushed back on the application of large parts of the constitution, including those referring to fundamental rights and citizenship, to Jammu and Kashmir as a means of bargaining for a special status for the state in the Indian constitution (Das 1971: 301–10).

The result, Article 370 of the Indian constitution, preserved Jammu and Kashmir's autonomy in that it allowed the state to have its own constitution that would be drafted by its constituent assembly (which was convened in 1951);[7] this body could also decide whether it wanted to accede to India in any further subjects beyond the three. Changes and additions to the article could be made by the president of India as long as they had the concurrence of the state assembly (Raghavan 2010: 148).[8] Besides the constitution, Jammu and Kashmir could also have its own flag and its head of state would have the title of prime minister.[9]

A smooth relationship between Delhi and Srinagar did not, however, ensue in the following years. The heightening tensions with Pakistan, with the Anglo-American bloc at least tacitly supporting Pakistan's claim; Abdullah's continued insistence on deposing the Maharaja; Pakistan's effective propaganda labelling

Abdullah an Indian puppet and his regime ineffectual and tyrannical (see Khan 1965: 147–50); and the growing dissensions within the National Conference itself, with different factions jostling for power ensured a steady decline in the relationship in the early 1950s. Jammu's Praja Parishad movement against Abdullah's regime, in particular, which had reached a frenzy by 1952, seriously complicated Delhi's already strained relationship with Srinagar. Added to this were demands from Ladakh for greater autonomy from the state government, which was regarded as discriminatory against Ladakhi interests.

The Delhi Agreement, reached between the Indian government and Abdullah's regime in July 1952, was an attempt to stem this tide. Reaffirming some of the principles of Article 370, it limited the central government's authority to the three subjects and granted state residents Indian citizenship, but allowed their rights and privileges to be determined by the state assembly based on the state's constitution. The state assembly had the right to recommend the head of state, who would be recognized by the president of India. And finally, Delhi could intervene and implement emergency powers only if requested by the state's assembly (Raghavan 2010: 218–21).

Rather than strengthening the political bonds between India and Kashmir, the agreement became a lightning rod around which Abdullah and his critics hardened their positions. Although Abdullah hailed the agreement, its implementation was put on hold until the drafting of the state constitution was completed by the constituent assembly. The assembly, meanwhile, was fraying at the seams as the disagreements among National Conference members came to the fore, making the job of the drafting committee almost impossible. As the Praja Parishad demanded the implementation of the agreement and Delhi pushed Abdullah to do the same, he dug his heels in and refused to comply, resorting instead to incendiary speeches demanding that the Maharaja be deposed. Over the course of the next year, as he grew suspicious of Delhi's motives and its support for him, Abdullah's speeches and stance towards India became increasingly implacable, and his calls for Kashmir's independence more insistent (Korbel 1954: 288–90).

Throughout the period from late 1947 to 1953, the Indian government chose to turn a blind eye to the situation on the ground in Kashmir, in particular to people's discontent with their government, and kept an unpopular regime propped up in the hope that it would deliver Kashmir to India in the event of a plebiscite. At the same time, as doubts about Abdullah's position grew, it cultivated an alternative leadership in his deputy, Bakshi Ghulam Muhammad, as a buffer in case Abdullah failed to toe India's line. Meanwhile, the Indian, especially right-wing, press incessantly questioned Abdullah's loyalty to India, reporting widely on the Praja Parishad agitation and the regime's poor handling of the situation. Anti-Abdullah and anti-Nehru sentiment reached a crescendo after the death of the Bharatiya Jan Sangh leader and supporter of the Parishad agitation, Shyama Prasad Mookerjee, who died while in the custody of the Jammu and Kashmir government in June 1953.

This, along with his speeches in favour of independence, made Abdullah a liability for the Indian government. He had, in a sense, outlived his usefulness, since by this time India had steadily moved away from plebiscite as a viable option to resolve the Kashmir issue and no longer needed him to deliver the Valley to India in the event of a plebiscite. It is no surprise, then, that at this point the Indian government abandoned Abdullah and gave its imprimatur for his removal. Abdullah was deposed and arrested in an internal coup on 9 August 1953, to be replaced by Bakshi as prime minister.

The dispute between India and Pakistan, both regionally and internationally, defined and ultimately overwhelmed the first regime of Jammu and Kashmir, whose relationship to the people of the state and to India foundered on the irresolution of this issue. Caught between India–Pakistan and its people, the regime resorted to crushing all legitimate dissent and rendering Jammu and Kashmir, in effect, into a one-party state. India, for its part, by not encouraging, indeed actively thwarting, democratic processes in Jammu and Kashmir, whose residents were Indian citizens, but only in name, saddled itself with a deeply politically discontented populace that would eventually rise up against it.

Indian Jammu and Kashmir, 1953–89

The dye had been cast in Jammu and Kashmir's relationship with India. The three and a half decades between Abdullah's ouster and arrest and the rise of the organized insurgency against the Indian state saw a deepening crisis of the Kashmiri polity. A succession of quisling governments kept themselves in power through corruption, nepotism, and by stifling all voices of dissent and opposition. The dispute continued to cast a long shadow on the state's internal politics, as the idea of Kashmir as an integral part of India became the only acceptable mantra; being anti-government meant being labelled anti-India. After directing a movement for plebiscite from house arrest outside Kashmir for over two decades through an organization called the Plebiscite Front, Abdullah himself returned to power with India's blessing in 1975. At the time of his death in 1982, the hopes of self-determination for Kashmiris had all but been dashed and Kashmir stood at the threshold of armed revolt.

The post-1953 regimes in Jammu and Kashmir, led by Bakshi (1953–63), Shamsuddin (1963–4), Sadiq (1964–71), and Mir Qasim (1971–5), undertook the task of constitutionally integrating the state into India, thus affirming while at the same time eroding Article 370. The state constituent assembly ratified the state's accession to India in 1954 and adopted the state constitution in 1956, which confirmed Article 370 as the basis of the state's relationship to India. However, over the years, the state legislature amended the constitution to chip away at the state's special status (Tremblay 2018: 228–9). By 1966, the powers of the president of India to impose president's rule on the state based on articles 356 and 357 of the Indian constitution were applicable to the state; the terms 'Sadr-i-Riyasat' and 'prime minister' had been amended to 'governor' and 'chief minister'; and Jammu and Kashmir could participate directly in elections to the Indian Lok Sabha.

As Pakistan grew ever closer to the United States of America, India officially abandoned its policy of supporting plebiscite and poured large amounts of economic aid into the state to support its governments, with the objective of wooing Kashmiris away from politics and towards economic development. This brought economic prosperity, but also had the effect of creating a Kashmiri Muslim middle class—a process that had already been underway during Abdullah's regime—that demanded economic parity with the new government-linked elites, an outlet for dissent, and expected its political urges to be satisfied. Abdullah, now a champion of plebiscite, became the representative of their demands and their denial by the state government and the Indian state. He was also elevated to the status of a martyr for the cause of Kashmiri self-determination in Pakistan, which had not so long before vilified him as an Indian stooge.

Deep political discontent finally spilled over in 1963 over the disappearance of the Prophet's hair from the Hazratbal shrine. This not only led to the toppling of the Bakshi government, but also provided the context for the emergence of multiple political groups—such as the Awami Action Committee, led by the Mirwaiz Kashmir—willing to express Kashmiris' political grievances. Abdullah was released in 1964 under the Sadiq government, and for a brief moment it looked as though he would prove to be a conduit for peace between India and Pakistan over Kashmir. Nehru's death dashed those hopes and any room for compromise not just between the two governments, but also within the state itself, where any opposition to the government's move to merge the National Conference with the Indian Congress party was dealt with fierce repression. By 1965, Abdullah was yet again under house arrest, this time in the southern Indian city of Kodaikanal.

Gauging that the situation in the Valley was to its advantage in 1965, Pakistan sent troops to infiltrate Kashmir with the intention of inciting and supporting an internal uprising against the Indian state. This did not come to pass and instead precipitated a full-scale war between India and Pakistan, which ended in an UN-brokered ceasefire. The war further intensified state suppression of political groups and activity in Kashmir, with large-scale arrests of members of the Plebiscite Front and the Awami Action Committee and the declaration of the Front as an unlawful organization.[10] Attempts to broker a peaceful solution led by Indian leaders such as J.P. Narayan and C. Rajagopalachari were ongoing behind the scenes, however.

These consistent efforts, and India's decisive victory over Pakistan in the Bangladesh War of 1971, pushed the Indian government and Abdullah towards a settlement. The result was the Kashmir Accord of 1974, between Indian prime minister Indira Gandhi and Abdullah, with his return to power as the chief minister of the state in 1975 with the support of the state Congress party. Although Abdullah pledged loyalty to India at the outset, his politics changed to a pro-autonomy stance as it became clear that the state Congress party was unwilling to support his policies. It was also evident that Kashmiris were in no mood for compromise and wanted him, as champion of self-determination, to take a stand against integrative politics. Despite this, many Kashmiris saw him as a traitor to the cause for signing the accord with India, and this, coupled with ever greater corruption and nepotism during his regime, led to deepening anger among middle-class Kashmiri Muslims, especially the youth.[11]

Abdullah's death precipitated a crisis within the National Conference as his family squabbled over control of the party and the Indian government intervened directly to take charge of the politics of the state. At first it supported the ascension of Abdullah's son and successor, Farooq Abdullah, to the office of chief minister, then removed him and installed his rival and Abdullah's son-in-law, G.M. Shah, instead. Farooq Abdullah returned to power in 1987 through the Farooq–Rajiv Accord, which established a National Conference–Congress coalition government in the state. The subsequent state legislative assembly elections, fought jointly by the National Conference and Congress, were massively rigged to ensure their victory and the loss of the Muslim United Front (MUF) coalition that included a number of political parties

133

such as the Jamaat-i-Islami (Tremblay 2018: 229). This proved to be the last straw for Kashmiris, and two years later, the Valley was engulfed in a violent insurgency.

The dispute between India and Pakistan continued to shape the politics of Jammu and Kashmir in the post-1953 period, placing it in a distinct position within India as a state, but not quite like any other in the country. India's relationship to Kashmir can be described as 'postcolonial colonialism' (Sökefeld 2005), with the centre keeping in place vassal governments that did its bidding and repressed all dissent. This involved a complex mix of coercion, collaboration, subjugation, and resistance on the part of India and the regimes as well as people that it sought to control. The secular, nationalist narrative on the basis of which India claimed this Muslim-majority state rang hollow within Kashmir itself, and gradually within India too. Kashmiri Muslims in particular increasingly felt that while Kashmir was good enough to be a part of India, they, as Muslims, were not good enough to enjoy the freedom to participate in its democratic system of government, thus alienating them from India altogether.

Moreover, with their focus directed towards controlling the politics of the Kashmir Valley, successive state governments continued to neglect the needs of Jammu and Ladakh, where mis-governance and venality ran rampant, and resentment towards Kashmir-centred governments grew rapidly, intensifying internal divides that further complicated the situation in the state. Even as institutional rot set in and Kashmir gradually descended into hell in these decades, Indians were being taught to consume it as a paradise on earth, a tourist destination par excellence, and a symbol embodying the innocence and purity of India.[12]

Azad Jammu and Kashmir

Although declared by the Poonch rebels to be free from Dogra rule and in existence on 24 October 1947, Azad Kashmir officially became part of Pakistan with the drawing of the Ceasefire Line between India and Pakistan on 1 January 1949. Thereafter, the status of this sliver of territory in northeast Pakistan has been determined, much like Jammu and Kashmir in India, in large part by the two states' stand on the Kashmir dispute. Pakistan cannot accept Azad Kashmir as a de jure part of itself without giving up its official claim to the entire territory of the erstwhile princely state. As a result, it has in practice institutionally integrated Azad Kashmir, but in theory does not recognize it as a province of Pakistan. This has created an ambiguous situation where Azad Kashmir, which wants to be a de jure province of Pakistan, is denied this official status, and thus has no political representation in the

Pakistani government or parliament. At the same time, it is not considered autonomous either, but rather a 'local authority', whose internal affairs are controlled and dictated by Pakistan, until such time as the Kashmir dispute is resolved through a plebiscite and the unfinished partition completed (Rose 1992: 236).

In the case of both the Indian and Pakistani parts of Jammu and Kashmir, thus, official or unofficial political integration has not been accompanied by the conferral of attendant political rights on their inhabitants. On the geographical and social margins of the states and yet so central to their nationalist imaginations, both have been simultaneously included into and excluded from their respective nation–states in significant ways. The primary difference between them is that while the Muslims of the Valley have risen up against India through the decades to demand their right to self-determination, the inhabitants of Azad Kashmir have not coalesced into an organized movement against Pakistan, although they have negotiated and resisted its interventions in multiple ways.

The early tension between the Pakistani state and the Azad government grew out of the latter's desire to be recognized as the legitimate government of the entire state of Jammu and Kashmir, with the authority to bring this state under Pakistan's control. However, not wanting any challenge to its own authority on

Kashmir, and in order to uphold its international commitment to settle the Kashmir issue through a plebiscite, Pakistan demoted Azad Kashmir to a local government under its own watchful eye. Once the ceasefire went into effect, the Pakistani army entered Azad areas and not only absorbed the Azad Army, but also prevented the disaffected Kashmiris from rising up against Pakistan in the 1950s as disillusionment regarding the resolution of the Kashmir issue began to set in. Also in 1949, the Pakistani government set up the Ministry of Kashmir Affairs (MKA) to direct and manage the government of Azad Kashmir, the responsibilities of which, as a result, were reduced to local administration (Snedden 2018: 119–20).

The Muslim Conference, although on paper in charge of the government, since its leader was the 'supreme head of state' with the power to appoint the President of Azad Kashmir, was quickly rendered powerless by the MKA due to the internal divisions within the party. Ghulam Abbas, who became the head of state of Azad Kashmir, and Sardar Ibrahim Khan, the first president of Azad Kashmir, did not see eye to eye. While the former wanted Jammu and Kashmir to be reunited and liberated, the latter wanted to develop democratic forms of governance within Azad Kashmir itself (Khan 1965: 111–13). Mirwaiz Yusuf Shah, who had left Srinagar for Azad Kashmir in 1947, formed yet another faction within the party, around whom the few Kashmiri Muslims in Azad Kashmir coalesced. Each faction attempted to limit the other's power by ingratiating itself with the MKA, thereby bringing Azad Kashmir further within the ambit of the Pakistani state (Snedden 2018: 123–4).

Since 1949, Azad Kashmir has been headed by several presidents, who have come to power on the basis of multiple political systems and varying arrangements with Pakistan (Snedden 2018: 124–6). As Snedden points out, over the years, candidates for elections in Azad Kashmir are increasingly aligned with Pakistan's position and the position of its mainstream political parties on Kashmir, and its party politics mirrors party politics in Pakistan, with the local affiliate of the national ruling party usually coming to power in the region. Local parties that are against the state's accession to Pakistan, such as the JKLF (Jammu Kashmir Liberation Front), are constitutionally banned from participating in any electoral contest (Schild 2015: 307; Snedden 2018: 125–6).

Pakistan undoubtedly controls Azad Kashmir's internal and external affairs, and there has been a fair bit of agreement on significant issues between the Pakistani state and successive Azad governments. Both endorse the same stand on the Kashmir issue—its resolution through a plebiscite, leading to the accession of the entire state to Pakistan. However, this has not precluded either Azad politicians or people from expressing their discontent with the Pakistani government over several issues. The most pressing issue, not surprisingly, is a desire for more autonomy to run the affairs of Azad Kashmir, as well as its inclusion, especially in the early years, in international negotiations and agreements on Kashmir (Rose 1992: 245). In addition, Azad governments resent their financial dependence on Islamabad. This could be mitigated by receiving royalties on the hydel power generated by the Mangla Dam, for instance, but the Pakistani state has been unwilling to do so (Rose 1992: 245; Snedden 2018: 128).

Another matter of controversy between the Pakistani state and Azad Kashmir governments is the status of Gilgit–Baltistan (formerly the Northern Areas), which Pakistan has administered since 1947. Azad Kashmir governments have claimed this region and demand that it be incorporated into Azad Kashmir since it was a part of erstwhile Jammu and Kashmir (Rose 1992: 250; Snedden 2018: 146–8). Added to this is the fact that despite the Azad government's official stand for the state's unification and accession to Pakistan, Azad Kashmir was the centre of the movement for the state's independence from both India and Pakistan.[13] Groups such as the JKLF and the lesser-known Kashmir Liberation Cell were located in and operated from this region, and were supported by the large Azad Kashmiri diaspora in the United Kingdom, consisting largely of the Mirpuris who had been displaced as a result of the Mangla Dam project (Snedden 2012: 184–5, 194–5; Rose 1992: 245, 251).

These lines of disagreement, particularly disgruntlement at Pakistan's hegemony in financial and political matters over Azad Kashmir, came to the fore in the wake of the reconstruction efforts after the earthquake that devastated large parts of Azad Kashmir in 2005. Indeed, as Pascale Schild argues, the tensions between the Pakistani reconstruction bureaucracy and the Azad government is illustrative of Pakistan's ambivalent, even duplicitous, relationship with Azad Kashmir. Pakistan's master plan for the region's reconstruction included the marginalization of the Azad government, with the ultimate aim of strengthening Pakistani dominance over the region rather than aiding reconstruction itself (Schild 2015).

In general, the conflict between India and Pakistan over Kashmir has cast a long shadow on the lives of the inhabitants of Azad Kashmir, especially those living along the border, through violence, displacement, and separation.[14] In some ways similar to the relationship between India and Jammu and Kashmir, the relationship between Pakistan and Azad Kashmir too is defined by domination on the one hand, and collaboration/integration as well as a push towards autonomy on the other. The main point of difference is that Jammu and Kashmir has representation in the Indian parliament, while Azad Kashmir does not have concomitant representation in Pakistan. Operating within the framework of the Kashmir dispute, Pakistan has not officially recognized Azad Kashmir as a province of Pakistan, while at the same time directing its political and economic affairs through what is essentially a patron–client relationship. Local state and non-state actors, however, have challenged the terms of this relationship and sometimes also Pakistan's position on the Kashmir dispute upon which it is premised.

Gilgit–Baltistan

The Kashmir dispute has rendered Gilgit–Baltistan, which was referred to as the Northern Areas until 2009, into an especially bordered and liminal region within Pakistan. Directly ruled by the national government through its agents, but lacking official status as a province as a result of which its inhabitants cannot participate in national elections, Gilgit–Baltistan exists on the metaphorical and literal periphery of the state. Moreover, its relationship to the dispute itself remains unclear, as its inhabitants do not consider themselves

Kashmiris nor their region a part of Jammu and Kashmir, and thus do not want its status to be determined on the basis of the dispute. Pakistan, however, at least on paper, considers Gilgit–Baltistan as part of the dispute, and has not legally integrated the region because it does not want to jeopardize its claim to the entire state by doing so. This liminality has produced a distinct sense of national belonging among the people of the region and a concomitant expression of their grievances and sense of alienation from the Pakistani state.

Historically, Gilgit was only tenuously connected to the princely state of Jammu and Kashmir, and that too through the British, who had established the Gilgit Agency in the late nineteenth century to direct political affairs in the region. The British returned the Gilgit Agency to the Maharaja of Jammu and Kashmir on 30 July 1947, much to the chagrin of the local population and the Gilgit Scouts, the local paramilitary force through which the British had maintained their control in the region. The situation came to a head once the news reached Gilgit that the Maharaja had acceded the state to India, leading to a revolt of the Gilgit Scouts against the Dogra functionary in the region and the establishment of a provisional government that requested Pakistan to accept its accession on 1 November 1947, which it has yet to do. The Scouts then set about liberating neighbouring principalities from the suzerainty of Dogra rule, including Baltistan, which was incorporated into Gilgit in August 1948 (Sökefeld 2018: 133–6).[15]

The provisional government itself did not last long, however, as the Pakistani political agent who came in to take charge of the area on 16 November 1947 did not brook any opposition to his authority (Bangash 2010: 132–3). He soon took over as military commander, taking charge of the Scouts as well as the administration, and made no effort to put an end to the exploitative practices such as forced labour and heavy taxes that had been in place prior to 1947. As people became increasingly restive and even began to protest against the new administration, their demands were squelched in true colonial fashion, this time in the name of Islam and the unity of the Pakistani nation. The Scouts served the authority in power, just as they had the British, even if that meant turning against their own people. The British political agent was replaced by a Pakistani one and business carried on as usual, with very little power devolving into local hands or local institutions. Accordingly, Sökefeld argues, Pakistan's attitude towards and relationship with this region should be characterized as a form of colonialism; Pakistan squandered whatever legitimacy it had in 1947 and forcefully maintained its rule (Sökefeld 2005: 959–60, 963).

This relationship has changed somewhat since 2009, when the Pakistan government introduced a new reform package whereby the now renamed Gilgit–Baltistan received a legislative assembly with limited powers and other institutions resembling those in Pakistan's provinces. However, the people continued to be denied the franchise. Thus, the inhabitants of this region are not quite citizens of Pakistan, since although they get regional representation and access to the High Court they do not have representation at the national level or access to the Supreme Court of Pakistan. At the same time, they are also not state subjects of Jammu and Kashmir, a legal right that is afforded to the inhabitants of Azad Kashmir. Constitutionally, thus, Gilgit–Baltistan is neither a part of Jammu and Kashmir, nor a part of Pakistan, but is still a part of the Kashmir dispute (Kreutzmann 2015: 177–8; Sökefeld 2015b: 176–7; Sökefeld 2018).

Gilgit–Baltistan's relationship with Azad Kashmir itself has been a complicated one. As noted earlier, Pakistan does not want the Azad Kashmir government to have control over Gilgit–Baltistan's affairs, but many Azad activists see Gilgit–Baltistan as an integral part of Jammu and Kashmir and hence demand its administrative integration into Azad Kashmir. Pakistan's government further endeavours to keep the two entities apart so as to better manage both by drawing a border—that is neither provincial nor international—between them (Sökefeld 2015b: 185). Within Gilgit–Baltistan itself, the support for incorporation into Azad Kashmir is divided along sectarian lines. Sunni politicians support it, since Sunnis are a minority in Gilgit but a majority in Azad Kashmir, while Shia politicians are against it, since they are a majority in Gilgit but would be a minority in an integrated Azad Kashmir and Gilgit–Baltistan (Sökefeld 2018: 140–1). Instead, Shia politicians regularly demand an incorporation of Gilgit–Baltistan into Pakistan as its fifth province (Sökefeld 2015b: 179).

For a majority of the people of Gilgit–Baltistan, there is little desire to be a part of any part of Jammu and Kashmir—an entity their forefathers led a freedom movement against. As Kreutzmann's notes, 'From the Gilgit–Baltistan viewpoint, both Kashmirs [Indian and Pakistani] seem to be entities that should be kept at a distance in order to allow self-determined participation in state affairs' (Kreutzmann 2015: 277). A recent survey of young people from Gilgit–Baltistan found that 82 per cent dissociate themselves from a Kashmiri identity and consider themselves Pakistanis instead (Sökefeld 2018: 145). It is also important to note, however, that there is a strand of nationalism in Gilgit–Baltistan that identifies it as a separate nation altogether and demands its independence from both Jammu and Kashmir and Pakistan (Sökefeld 2015b: 179).

Much like Azad Kashmir, Gilgit-Baltistan is both marginalized institutionally and otherwise, and yet central to Pakistan's vision of itself as a Muslim state in South Asia, a vision that remains incomplete in the absence of the state of Jammu and Kashmir. This explains why it has been so imperative for Pakistan to maintain control over the region and its resources, while at the same time denying its people any measure of self-representation and a voice in running their own affairs, or indeed the affairs of the country in which they are a not-quite-province. Pakistani maps show Gilgit-Baltistan as part of the territories of Pakistan, but not Azad Kashmir, which is shown as a part of Jammu and Kashmir, while neither is referred to as the state's territory in the Pakistani constitution. It is deeply ironic that the entity from which the Gilgit Scouts declared independence in November 1947—Jammu and Kashmir—continues to determine the fate of Gilgit-Baltistan and its people, while the entity that they chose to accede to—Pakistan—refuses, to this day, to grant constitutional recognition to them or their territory as an equal province of Pakistan.

India and Pakistan have a single point of agreement, albeit unstated, when it comes to the Kashmir issue: neither wants an independent Kashmir on its borders, which both consider a threat to their strategic interests in the region. Thus, by bordering its constituent parts while also drawing borders between them—some of which have no legal meaning and yet control their inhabitants' physical and political movements—India and Pakistan have been successful in partitioning Jammu and Kashmir and preventing an effective challenge to their state interests.

Notes

1. Kishtwari, Singh, and Krishan (undated: 19).
2. Hindu-majority India claims the Muslim-majority state of Jammu and Kashmir to prove its ideological commitment to secularism, while Pakistan's claim rests on its self-definition as the homeland for the Muslims of South Asia, according to which the state rightfully belongs within Pakistan. The strategic interests of both are tied to control over this region. For the Indo-Pak dispute over Kashmir, see Ganguly (1997, 2003, 2016); Behera (2006); Zutshi (2017); Thomas (1992).
3. Interview with *The Scotsman*, 14 April 1949 (Das 1971: 266–8).
4. Speech on 27 February 1948 (Kishtwari, Singh, and Krishan undated: 9).
5. For the UN's involvement in the Indo-Pak dispute, see Raghavan (2010), chapters 4 and 6, and Behera (2006). For UN documents, see Das (1971: 345–57).

6. Moreover, one of Pakistan's demands was that plebiscite could not be held until Abdullah's government was disbanded or removed. In addition, Abdullah did not want to include his political adversaries into the interim Kashmir administration after the plebiscite had been held (Raghavan 2010: 117).

7. For the Indian Constituent Assembly debates on Article 370, see Rai (2018a).

8. On Article 370 and its consequences, see Noorani (2011).

9. This special status became the basis of the Praja Parishad agitation in Jammu, with its slogan, 'One Flag, One Constitution, One Premier'. Ladakh, too, was in favour of the state's accession to and integration into India, and demanded greater control over its administrative affairs within Jammu and Kashmir.

10. On post-1953 Kashmiri politics, and the 1965 war, see Hussain (undated: chs 3–5).

11. On 1970s and 1980s Kashmiri youth culture and its views on Abdullah, India, and Pakistan, see Faheem (2018).

12. On this point, see Kabir (2009).

13. According to Sökefeld, a recent survey has shown that, '44 percent of the people in AJK [Azad Jammu and Kashmir] are not content with the political status quo, but favor the independence of J&K instead' (2015b: 178).

14. See Mahmud (2018: 211–29). On the LOC's impact on the Indian side, see Hans (2004); Gupta (2014).

15. On the situation up to this moment, see Bangash (2010: 132–3).

7

The Kashmir Insurgency

Shaheed [martyr] Dr. Mohammad Rafi gave his Life
for Our Freedom

—Banner, University of Kashmir, 2018[1]

This banner, which flutters in the breeze on the
building that houses the departments of Sociology and
Political Science at the University of Kashmir, signifies
the latest manifestation of the insurgency against the
Indian state that began in the Kashmir Valley in 1989.
Covering as it does the board of the 'Department of
Political Science', the banner encapsulates how politics
and its study have become synonymous with resistance
to Indian occupation in the Kashmir Valley. Described
as the 'Kashmiri intifada' in recent scholarship, this form
of protest began in the second decade of this century,
as Kashmiri Muslim youth took to the streets, pelting

stones and demanding azaadi (freedom) from India and its brutal military regime. It was also accompanied by an efflorescence of literary and artistic productions, and a celebration of martyrdom, which challenge broader Indian hegemony over history, memory, and politics in Kashmir (see Kak 2013b; Kaul 2015; Duschinski, Bhan, Zia, and Mahmood 2018).

This intifada is in many ways a direct product of the response of the Indian state to the insurgency that emerged in 1989, which was itself the culmination of decades of Indian misrule in the state. Rather than engaging with the significant issues raised by the insurgents, the Indian state chose to clamp down militarily, rendering the Kashmir Valley into one of the most militarized zones in the world. The current generation of youth at the forefront of the intifada came of age surrounded by the tyrannies of the Indian army, their everyday lives suffused with news of disappearances, torture, rapes, and extra-judicial killings of their loved ones and friends, not to mention the trauma of daily humiliations and the impossibility of being able to conduct life in the face of an endless cycle of strikes, curfews, and retaliations.

This chapter charts the various phases of the insurgency that have defined the politics, society, and culture of the Kashmir Valley for the past three decades. It argues that the resistance to the Indian state has grown and changed over the decades, with demands for azaadi taking on multiple meanings, from plebiscite, to freedom from injustice and tyranny, to outright independence. By choosing to blame Pakistan for what now appears to be a full-scale rebellion in the Valley, rather than accepting some culpability for the situation and attempting to arrive at a resolution of the issues plaguing the state through negotiations, the Indian and the regional governments of Jammu and Kashmir have effectively lost control of the Valley. Since Islam has become an oppositional identity for Kashmiri Muslims against the Indian state, the issue has taken on religious overtones, especially in an era of Hindu extremism, but it is important to not lose sight of the profound political grievances that continue to undergird this insurgency.

The First Phase, 1989–2000

Kashmiris had been mobilizing against India (and Pakistan in the case of Azad Kashmir), for decades prior to 1989. Several organizations, such as the Plebiscite Front, the Awami Action Committee, and student groups such as the Student and Youth League as well as cross-border groups such as Al-Fateh, carried out non-violent and violent campaigns for Kashmiri self-determination throughout the period from the

1950s into the 1980s (Tremblay 2018: 235–7). These movements were spurred by the political situation in Jammu and Kashmir after Sheikh Abdullah's dismissal and detention in 1953, which, as we have seen, was followed by a series of puppet regimes that, in consort with the Indian state, relentlessly chipped away at Kashmir's autonomy within the Indian union. India, meanwhile, poured financial aid into the state in the vain hope that it would bully Kashmiris into forgetting their political disenfranchisement in favour of economic well-being. This had the opposite effect, however, since it created a new class of prosperous elites that benefited from their association with the regime, while the middle-classes and the masses toiled away with no hope for advancement. As the gap between those who controlled power and resources and those who had to fight for access to even basic services increased, so did political alienation and discontent.[2]

By the time Farooq Abdullah took over the reins of the government after his father's death in 1982, Kashmir was already ripe for a mass revolt. This was given the final push by the central government's policies of direct intervention in Kashmiri politics, including the removal of Farooq Abdullah and his brother-in-law, G.M. Shah, as chief minister in quick succession, followed by the reinstatement of Farooq Abdullah as head of state in 1987. This coalition government of the state party, the

National Conference, and the national party, the Congress, had to be maintained at all cost, even if it meant massively rigging the March 1987 state assembly elections to ensure the defeat of the 11-party opposition organization, the MUF. As it turned out, this was a pyrrhic victory for the Government of India, because it won the election, but lost Kashmir in the process.

By 1989, a full-scale armed insurgency led by two political organizations—the Jammu and Kashmir Liberation Front (JKLF) and Hizbul Mujahideen—spilled over onto the streets of the major cities of the Valley. The two organizations emerged in the wake of the 1987 elections, through the efforts of and led by two members of the erstwhile MUF, Yasin Malik and Syed Mohammad Yusuf Shah, both of whom had been arrested for their participation in the elections.[3] Although the two organizations differed in their objectives—with the JKLF seeking complete autonomy for Kashmir, while Hizbul sought its integration into Pakistan—in the early years they joined hands to demand azaadi from India. In 1993, almost 30 separatist and militant organizations—including the People's Conference and the Jamaat-i-Islami—representing the complete spectrum of ideologies on the Kashmir issue and its resolution came together to form the All Parties Hurriyat Conference (APHC) (Chowdhary 2002: 2400).

The separatist movement received mass support from a cross-section of Kashmiri society, with otherwise apolitical men, women, and children joining massive demonstrations to protest decades of misrule in the region. Hundreds of young men, eager to make their contribution to the cause in the tradition of the Afghan *mujahideen* (guerilla fighters), slipped across the border into Pakistan to receive arms and training.[4] The early years were heady with optimism for Kashmiris, as there was a genuine belief that azaadi was just around the corner.

India, however, took a radically different view of the situation and implemented immediate steps to deal with what it saw as an assault on its sovereignty in Kashmir. The Indian government suspended the regional government, imposed president's rule over the state, and brought the full might of its military and border security forces to bear on quelling the insurgency. As the insurgency came to be increasingly hijacked by outside forces by the mid- to late 1990s, with Pakistani-supported organizations such as Harkat-ul-Mujahideen, Jaish-e-Muhammad, and Lashkar-i-Taiba seeking to use this as an opportunity to destabilize India (Chowdhary 2002: 2398–9), India ratcheted up its military response accordingly. It made no distinction between the homegrown indigenous revolt and the external forces using it as a means to further their own agenda of global jihad. Search and seizure operations, disappearances (especially of young men), torture, arson, murder, and rape by Indian security forces became the order of the day.[5]

The insurgency and counter-insurgency as well as the criminal elements that proliferated as law and order disintegrated and guns became readily available had a devastating impact on Kashmiri society. Violence engulfed the Valley, with targeted assassinations and kidnappings of important political and academic figures by Kashmiri insurgents; bombings and other attacks by external groups; thefts and killings by local criminal gangs; and reprisals by Indian security forces. Kashmir became inhabitable for most Kashmiris as any semblance of community, civil society, and normalcy was replaced by terror, lawlessness, rumour, and suspicion. Many Kashmiris were forced to leave the Valley and the mass exodus in the first few years of the insurgency of Kashmiri Pandits, the minority community of Hindus,[6]—which felt increasingly targeted by local and external groups—further polarized Kashmiri society, this time along lines of religion. These developments subverted the popular nature of the insurgency, tarnishing the very real political grievances that underlay it with the brush of criminality and Islamic radicalism.

The fact that the insurgency was limited to the Kashmir Valley and was actively opposed by the other two regions of the state—Jammu and Ladakh—made it easier for the Indian government to deny the existence of a genuine mass movement and instead claim that a few disgruntled Muslim youth were being misled by the evil designs of Pakistan. Far from desiring autonomy from India, Jammu and Ladakhi politics was based on demands for autonomy from Kashmir and its repressive governments instead, and greater integration with India. For instance, the insurgency revived Ladakhi Buddhist insecurities about the Valley, leading to demands for Union Territory status for Ladakh, which ended with the establishment of the Ladakh Autonomous Hill Development Council in 1995.[7] The insurgency, thus, widened the divides among the sub-regions of Kashmir, the long-term repercussions of which on state politics are only recently becoming clearer.

Far from ushering in freedom, India's response to the insurgency transformed the Valley into a landscape of horrors, pockmarked with military encampments, army convoys, weapons caches, shuttered cinema halls and restaurants, buildings wrapped in barbed wire, and shattered bodies.

Second Phase, 2000–9

The insurgency had clearly reached a tipping point by 2000. Deep fatigue with its methods, if not its goals, had set in among the local population. The attack on the Indian parliament in December 2001, which was linked to two Pakistan-funded organizations that had been operating in Kashmir, Jaish-e-Muhammad and Lashkar-i-Taiba, further diverted attention away from the indigenous Kashmiri resistance and its demands. In addition, the Indian government had begun to push for a reinstatement of the electoral process that would restore good governance and civil society to the deeply wounded society. These factors allowed for mainstream political parties, such as the NC and the People's Democratic Party (PDP), which emerged in 1998, to campaign on the basis of good governance, and in the case of the PDP, to acknowledge the demands of separatist groups. At the same time, this context created a space for the emergence of moderate voices within separatist organizations such as the APHC, thus making rapprochement on the issue a real possibility for the first time since the start of the insurgency. By the end of the decade, however, for a variety of reasons, these hopes had been shattered and a more militant separatist politics reasserted itself.

Reeta Chowdhary Tremblay has argued that we need to tread carefully when analyzing Kashmiri participation in elections, which should not necessarily be equated with consent for Indian rule. She notes that for the past six decades, Kashmiris have 'modulated their responses to the elected governments of Jammu and Kashmir between the poles of accommodation and resistance', at certain times participating in elections to ensure that their basic needs are met, and at other times contributing to movements that challenge the authority of the Indian state within Kashmir (Tremblay 2018: 223; see also Baba 2012). Separatist politics, in other words, can and does co-exist with the politics of governance in Kashmir.

After a decade of violence that brought little in terms of concrete gains towards self-determination, instead wrecking Kashmiri society from within, Kashmiris were, not surprisingly, attracted to the 'healing touch' agenda of the PDP. The PDP itself recognized the importance of appealing to the concerns of the populace, not just in terms of providing succour from the devastation of the past decade, but also sympathizing with their political demands for greater autonomy and self-determination. As a result, the state assembly elections in 2002 yielded a PDP–Congress coalition government, rotating the post of chief minister between them (Tremblay 2018: 230–1).

For a few years it seemed that Kashmir had turned a corner and peace had returned. This was further reflected in the marginalization of extremists within the separatist movement, as more centrist leaders such as Abdul Ghani Lone of the People's Conference within the APHC called for taking the movement in a new direction. Lone attempted to address some of the issues that had subverted the popular nature of the insurgency and tainted it, focusing instead on local political grievances that could be resolved through a political solution rather than militancy and global jihad. He also acknowledged the need to attend to the demands and concerns of the people of Jammu and Ladakh (Chowdhary 2002: 2398–9).

These revolutionary ideas led to Lone's assassination in 2002, and although the centrists continued to hold sway for a few more years, they were unable to consolidate their position within the APHC. The pro-Pakistani hardline elements represented by Jamaat-i-Islami's Ali Shah Geelani increasingly asserted themselves, making it difficult for the APHC to function as a united representative of Kashmiri aspirations.[8] The Indian government, for its part, did little to encourage the moderates, such as Mirwaiz Umar Farooq, rejecting their overtures for a dialogue and treating all separatists with mistrust and disdain (Editorial 2003: 3020–1).

By 2008, separatist politics was yet again on a collision course with the state government, which led to the government's collapse and the seizure of the political space by separatists. This happened in the context of the Amarnath agitation that emerged when the Government of India and the state government reached an agreement to divert some 99 acres of forest land in the Kashmir Valley to the Amarnath Shrine Board for the construction of shelters for pilgrims on their way to the Amarnath shrine. This decision evoked deep fears amongst Kashmiri Muslims of land grabs by Hindus and led to the organization of massive demonstrations to protest the order in the Kashmir Valley. This was followed by the concomitant organization of protests by Hindu groups in Jammu, further deepening the divide between Jammu and the Valley. The issue gave voice to the political disgruntlements of the entire state and allowed for the consolidation of power by hardliners on both sides (Chowdhary 2014: 196).

This growing divide, embodied by the extremist separatists in the Valley and right-wing Hindu parties in Jammu, was apparent in the state's electoral politics as well, especially the results of the 2008 assembly elections. Based on its support of Kashmiri Muslim identity politics, the PDP registered gains in the Valley as well as in the Muslim districts of Jammu, and the Bharatiya Janata Party (BJP) made significant inroads in Jammu for the first time as a result of its backing of Hindu right-wing politics (Chowdhary 2014: 197). Although a NC–Congress combine was able to defeat the PDP and form the government in 2008, the continuing communalization and radicalization of politics in the intervening years, aided by rapidly intensifying political alienation, would bring the PDP and BJP back to power in an alliance in 2014. This took place in the context of an escalating separatist politics, which played a significant role in mobilizing Kashmiris, especially the youth, during this period.

Intifada, 2009–Present

It is important to remind ourselves of the deeply intertwined nature of separatist and electoral politics in the state of Jammu and Kashmir to understand how we arrived at the current situation in the Kashmir Valley. The participation by Kashmiris in elections, which has grown in recent years, does not imply a decline in separatist sentiments or involvement in separatist politics. Indeed, the last decade has yielded a new kind of resistance to the Indian state alongside new verdicts on the electoral landscape. The lack of resolution of the basic issues related to the insurgency and its impact, especially the continued presence and impunity of the Indian security forces in the Valley, blatant human rights violations within and outside the Valley, combined with rampant mis-governance, corruption, and the inability of state governments to provide basic services, has provided ample cause for young Kashmiri Muslim men and women to participate in the azaadi movement.

This has been exacerbated in the context of the rise of Hindu nationalism and anti-Muslim sentiment across India as a result of the BJP central government.

A series of events between 2009 and 2014 were critical in shaping this most recent iteration of homegrown Kashmiri resistance. These events collectively revealed the complicity of the state and central governments in covering up gross violations of the civil and human rights of Kashmiri citizens and thus their indifference to Kashmiri suffering. In 2009, for instance, the rape and murder of two Kashmiri women in Shopian, allegedly by Indian security forces, was mishandled by the state government, with the chief minister, Omar Abdullah, going so far as to deny that these were cases of rape at all. Later in the same year, mass graves of as many as 3,000 victims of the security forces and militants came to light across Kashmir. Again, Abdullah's government failed to move on providing genetic testing of the bodies to match them with disappeared persons (Tremblay 2018: 231).

These events provided the context for a series of protests that began in the summer of 2010, in the wake of the killing of three young men by security forces in a staged encounter in Baramulla. The demonstrations gathered steam as a young boy was killed by a tear gas shell during one of the protests, cascading into further demonstrations, clashes, and deaths. Despite the imposition of curfews, the government seemed to have lost control of the streets, because young people poured out into them and pelted stones (Tremblay 2018: 232). This was a different way of expressing anger at India, reclaiming the streets from its security forces through stones wielded by unarmed young men and some women, rather than through guns carried by militants. Social media exploded with messages and discussions about the street protests, informing Kashmiris about the location of the next one, while at the same time challenging the Indian government's and media's line on these being Pakistan-sponsored events. The emotions of these youth who had grown up surrounded by the insecurity of violence spilled over in protest poetry, letters, notes, and cartoons that gave voice to Kashmiri individual and collective trauma (Kak 2013a: xiv–xviii).

While the state government floundered in its response to this groundswell of public opinion against it, the Indian government relied on the time-honoured tactic of denying the legitimacy of the protests by labelling them the work of outsiders on the one hand, and waiting them out on the other. Although the stone-pelting incidents did subside by the end of 2010, not only had they set the tone for resistance in Kashmir, but resistance itself continued unabated on social media platforms; in strikes to commemorate the significant days in the history of the Kashmiri movement, organized by parties such as Geelani's Tehreek-e-Hurriyat; in funerals and other forms of public grieving on the streets for protest martyrs; and in the commemorations of the lives of these martyrs in graveyards (Tremblay 2018: 240–1). These spaces had existed since the first man was killed in the movement, but in the past decade they have become central to memorializing and thus continuing the movement after the end of violent insurgency (Junaid 2018: 249).

Afzal Guru's hanging by the Indian state in Tihar Jail in Delhi in February 2014, without informing his family, added to the growing list of the state's cruelties as well as the list of Kashmiri martyrs to the cause of freedom.[9] This time the state government took no chances and imposed a massive curfew in the Valley, but while this prevented immediate protests, it only heightened the resistance. This was followed by devastating floods in parts of the Kashmir Valley, especially Srinagar, in September 2014, to which the state government responded woefully inadequately, bungling relief efforts and not providing support for rebuilding. This time the Kashmiri populace responded electorally by defeating the NC at the polls in the late 2014 assembly elections (Tremblay 2018: 232).

However, the elections yielded a divided verdict across the state, with the PDP doing better than the NC in the Kashmir Valley but not well enough to form a government without a coalition partner, while the BJP emerged as the largest winner in Jammu but with no presence in the Valley (Tremblay 2018: 232–3; see also Tremblay and Bhatia 2015). The PDP–BJP partnership government formed in the wake of the elections in early 2015 institutionalized the Valley–Jammu divide, and being unable to fulfill its agenda of alliance that was meant to assuage Kashmiri Muslims through the delivery of good governance, collapsed in 2018.

This collapse was not just because of the vehemence of the most recent round of protests in the Kashmir Valley, which continue unabated to this moment, but because of the fundamentally conflicting views of the PDP and the BJP on Kashmir's status within the Indian union. While the PDP recognizes the necessity of Kashmir's autonomy, and thus the symbolism of Article 370, the BJP wants to revoke Kashmir's special status. By softening their stance on these issues and promising to work together, the two parties ensured that neither of their respective constituencies in the Kashmir Valley or Jammu was satisfied with the coalition government.

As a result, politics continued to radicalize in both regions, with separatists gaining ground in the Valley while Hindu extremists fanned the flames in Jammu. Issues such as the resettlement of Kashmiri Pandits in the Valley, a core promise of the BJP to this community, or the banning of beef, provided fodder for both sides to ignite their followers, and not surprisingly, were seen by Kashmiri Muslims as attacks on their very identity and well-being. These fears intensified at the death of PDP's leader, Mufti Muhammad Sayed, and the instatement of his daughter, Mehbooba Mufti, as chief minister, as Kashmiri Muslims doubted her ability to keep the BJP's worst tendencies in check (Tremblay 2018: 233–5).

So, in July 2016, when the Indian security forces killed a leader of the Hizbul Mujahideen and one of the most recognizable and celebrated faces of the resistance, a young man named Burhan Wani, Kashmiri youth once again erupted onto the streets, pelting stones and demanding azaadi. As the Indian state responded with characteristic brutality, blinding young people and bystanders with pellet guns and filling jails, Kashmiris vowed that this time they would not back down. Shuttering their shops and businesses, boycotting offices and workplaces, the older generation joined hands with their younger compatriots, willing to sacrifice livelihood and life, even the lives of their own children, for freedom. The resistance had been radicalized to such an extent that it had taken on a life of its own, beyond organizations that were regarded as too accommodative and beyond political solutions. For the young people on the streets, the only endpoints were, and continue to be, freedom or martyrdom.

As we have seen, Kashmiris have been celebrating their land as well as expressing their anger, frustration, and deep sorrow at its destruction through the narrative medium throughout their past. This continued during the insurgency, when a slew of poems captured their mood and recorded their traumas as the movement spiralled into a cycle of violence (Kaul 2015: 135–61). The most recent intifada has also found expression in poetry, not surprisingly especially in rap, to match its spontaneity and close relationship to the street. A well-known rapper, M.C. Kash, for instance, freestyles about the Kashmiri situation thus:

> Keep knocking on my door every night
> Looking for a rebel in the eyes of my child
> They're blind to the innocence
> Murder all the innocents
> Rising up to prominence
> Hiding all the evidence
> Scared of the dissidents
> The common sense is to
> Brutally suppress all voices or
> Shoot pellets to blind
> Keep knocking on my door every night … (Kash n.d.)

This is the cry not of a victim, but a rebel, mobilizing others to join the resistance.

As I write this in summer 2019, the mood is sullen, and alienation runs deep in Kashmir. Young people continue to join the resistance, are hunted down and killed, causing even more to join, and the cycle repeats itself. The case of Dr Mohammad Rafi Bhat, with whom this chapter began, is illustrative in this regard. An even more recent case in point is Adil Ahmad Dar's suicide attack on Indian security forces in Pulwama as a member of Lashkar-i-Taiba this past February. Although India labels these young men terrorists and militants, they are simply students, or professors, or shop owners, or clerks, among many, many other ordinary middle-class Kashmiris, who are fed up with the coercive power of the Indian state and its forces and want them gone. The call of the intifada is palpable and has little to do with economic or even political conditions in Kashmir; rather, it is driven by the idea of resisting India and regaining control of Kashmir from its security forces. As we have seen, electoral politics and separatist politics have co-existed in Kashmir since 1947, but it looks as though a particular kind of separatist politics has now gained ascendency.

Moderate voices appear to have been marginalized, as evident in the brutal assassination in June 2018 of journalist and editor of *Rising Kashmir*, Shujaat Bukhari, who refused to pander to extremist positions and urged for a negotiated settlement of the Kashmir issue.

The Pulwama bombing and its aftermath—with India and Pakistan coming close to a military confrontation, Narendra Modi's warmongering at the expense of Kashmiris to secure a second term as prime minster, the closing down of the main highway that runs through the Valley by the Indian army in the name of security, the suspension of state elections for the unforeseen future, and the harassment of Kashmiri Muslims across India—had already hardened positions to the point of no return.

And now, rather than using its second-term mandate to repair India's broken relationship with Kashmir, the BJP has decided to fulfil a long-standing campaign promise. By presidential decree, it has amended Article 370 that renders it null and void, making all provisions of the Indian Constitution applicable to Jammu and Kashmir. Further, it has pushed through a bill dismantling the state of Jammu and Kashmir into two union territories ruled directly by the centre: Jammu and Kashmir, and Ladakh.

To clamp down on protests, the Valley has been placed on military lockdown with no communications allowed in or out. The deep fear held by Kashmiri Muslims of demographic change in the Valley is now a real possibility as the constitutional amendments will allow any Indian citizen to own land in this union territory. The response in the Valley and outside to this move—which among other things is an attack on Indian federalism—remains to be seen. It has, however, proven beyond doubt that to the Indian state, and perhaps also to most Indian citizens, Kashmir is a mere territory devoid of people.

Notes

1. Dr Mohammad Rafi Bhat, newly appointed assistant professor of sociology at the University of Kashmir, was killed by Indian security forces in May 2018 within 40 hours of joining the militant organization Hizbul Mujahideen. Hundreds thronged to his funeral procession; his decision to join a militant organization and his quick death after doing so perfectly captures the current situation in the Kashmir Valley.

2. For the political economy of alienation in post-1953 Kashmir, see Hussain (undated: ch. 3).

3. Yasin Malik, head of the Islamic Students' League (a member organization of the MUF), did not participate in the 1987 elections, but he campaigned for Mohammad Yusuf Shah, who was running as an MUF candidate from the Amira Kadal constituency in Srinagar. Shah won the election by a landslide but his opponent from the NC was declared the winner, and both Malik and Shah were arrested for agitating against the results. After their release, Malik joined the JKLF, while Shah took the title of Syed Salahuddin and became the head of the Hizbul Mujahideen. See Bose (2003: 47–9).

4. On the motivations of these youth and the multiple meanings of 'jihad', see Robinson (2013).

5. The most well-known case of mass rape carried out by Indian security forces was in Kunan Poshpora in 1991. For more, see Batool, Butt, Mushtaq, Rashid, and Rather (2016). For the gendered nature of military violence in Kashmir, see Kazi (2018 and 2010).

6. On this displaced population, see Datta (2016).

7. On this and the attempts by the Indian state to incorporate Ladakh into its security apparatus, see Aggarwal and Bhan (2009), Wani (2014), and Gagnè (2017).

8. Geelani believes that the Kashmiri Muslim movement is not simply a political but a religious struggle that is part of the global movement of jihad; he also argues that Hindus and Muslims are two nations and has consistently advocated for Kashmir's merger with Pakistan. He broke away from the AHPC and formed his own organization, Tehreek-e-Hurriyat, in 2004 (Chowdhary 2002: 2399); on Geelani's ideas, see Sikand (2010).

9. Afzal Guru, a former Kashmiri militant at the time of the December 2001 attack on the Indian parliament, was implicated, tried, and sentenced to death for his involvement in the incident. For more, see Zia (2018).

Bibliography

Primary Sources

Abbas, Chaudhuri Ghulam. 1950. *Kashmakash*. Lahore: Urdu Akademy.

Abdullah, Sheikh Muhammad. 1946. *Quit Kashmir: Memorandum to the British Cabinet Mission*. Srinagar (pamphlet).

———. 1944. 'Introduction'. In *Naya Kashmir*. Srinagar: All Jammu and Kashmir National Conference.

Anonymous. 1875. *Kashmeer and Its Shawls*. London: Wyman & Sons.

Basati, Ghulam Muhammad. 1937. 'Kya Deen-i-Islam Mazhabi Dhakosla Hai?' New Delhi: Bhushan Bazaz Private Collection.

Bazaz–Gandhi–Nehru Correspondence. 1936. *The Hamdard*, 29 August.

Dutt, J.C. 1990 [1898]. *Kings of Kashmira: A Translation of the Sanskrita Work of Jonaraja, Shrivara and of Prajyabhatta and Shuka*, vol. III. New Delhi: Mittal Publications.

———. 1879. *Kings of Kashmira: Being a Translation of the Sanskrita Work Rajatarangini of Kahlana Pandita*, vol. I. Calcutta: Self-Published.

Fazl, Abul. 2004. *The Ain-i Akbari*. Translated from Persian by H. Blochmann, 2nd ed. edited by D.C. Phillott, vol. II. Lahore: Sang-E-Meel Publications.

Ghai, Ved Kumari. 1973. *Nilamata-Purana: A Critical Edition and English Translation*, vol. 2. Srinagar: Jammu and Kashmir Academy of Art, Culture, and Languages.

Kash, M.C. undated. https://www.youtube.com/watch?v=QfsV-J1U2kI (accessed 14 August 2018).

Kishtwari, Abdul Majid, Trilok Singh, and Maharaj Krishan, eds. Undated. *Irshadat-e-Baba-e-Quom*. Srinagar: Ghulam Muhammad and Sons.

Kraalwari, Maqbool Shah. 1913. *Pirnama*. Srinagar (pamphlet).

Lawrence, Walter R. 1996 [1895]. *The Valley of Kashmir*. Jammu: Kashmir Kitab Ghar.

'Meem'. 1938. 'Kashmir Mein Zimmedar Nizam-e-Hukumat ki Zarurat'. *The Hamdard*, 31 July: 55.

Raina, N.N. 1991. *Oral Transcript*, 2 vols. Acc. # 580. New Delhi: Nehru Memorial Museum and Library.

Pandit, R.S. 1968 [1935]. *Rajatarangini: The Saga of the Kings of Kasmir*. Translated from the original Samskrta and entitled the River of Kings with an Introduction, Annotations, Appendices, Index, etc. New Delhi: Sahitya Akademi.

Stein, M.A. 1979 [1900]. *Kalhana's Rajatarangini: A Chronicle of the Kings of Kasmir, Translated, with an Introduction,*

Commentary, & Appendices, 2 vols. Delhi: Motilal Banarsidass Publishers.

The Hamdard. 1938. 3 April and 31 July.

Wilson, H.H. 1825. 'An Essay on the Hindu History of Cashmir'. *Asiatic Researches*, XV: 1–119.

Secondary Sources

Aggarwal, Ravina, and Mona Bhan. 2009. '"Disarming Violence": Development, Democracy, and Security on the Borders of India'. *The Journal of Asian Studies*, 68 (2): 519–42.

Aitchison, C.U. 1983 [1929]. *A Collection of Treaties, Engagements and Sanads Relating to India and Neighboring Countries (revised and continued up to 1929)*. Vol. XII: *Jammu & Kashmir, Sikkim, Assam & Burma*. Delhi: Mittal Publications.

Alam, Muzaffar, and Sanjay Subrahmanyam. 2004. 'The Making of a Munshi'. *Comparative Studies of South Asia, Africa and the Middle East*, 24 (2): 61–72.

Alder, Gary. 1985. *Beyond Bokhara: The Life of William Moorcroft, Asian Explorer and Pioneer Veterinary Surgeon, 1767–1825*. London: Century Publications.

Asher, Catherine B. 1992. *Architecture of Mughal India*. Cambridge: Cambridge University Press.

Baba, Noor Ahmad. 2012. 'Democracy and Governance in Kashmir'. In *The Parchment of Kashmir: History, Society and Polity*, edited by Nyla Ali Khan, pp. 103–24. New York: Palgrave Macmillan.

Bamzai, P.N.K. 1980. *Kashmir and Central Asia*. New Delhi: Light and Life Publishers.

———. 1962. *A History of Kashmir: Political, Social, Cultural, From the Earliest Times to the Present Day*. Delhi: Metropolitan Book Co.

Banerjee, Paula. 2010. *Borders, Histories, Existences: Gender and Beyond*. New Delhi: Sage.

Bangash, Yaqoob Khan. 2010. 'Three Forgotten Accessions: Gilgit, Hunza and Nagar'. *The Journal of Imperial and Commonwealth History*, 38 (1): 117–43.

Batool, Essar, Ifrah Butt, Samreena Mushtaq, Munaza Rashid, and Natasha Rather. 2016. *Do You Remember Kunan Poshpora?* New Delhi: Zubaan.

Bayly, C.A. 1998. *Origins of Nationality in South Asia: Patriotism and Ethical Government in the Making of Modern India*. New Delhi: Oxford University Press.

Bazaz, Prem Nath. 1954. *The History of Struggle for Freedom in Kashmir, Cultural and Political, from the Earliest Times to the Present Day*. New Delhi: Kashmir Publishing Company.

———. 1934. *Kashmir Ka Gandhi*. Srinagar: Kashmir Publishing Company.

Behera, Navnita Chadha. 2006. *Demystifying Kashmir*. Washington, DC: Brookings Institution Press.

Bose, Sumantra. 2003. *Kashmir: Roots of Conflict, Paths to Peace*. Cambridge, MA: Harvard University Press.

Chishti, Vanessa. 2018. 'Producing Paradise: Kashmir's Shawl Economy, the Quest for Authenticity and the Politics of

Representation in Europe, c. 1770–1870'. In *Kashmir: History, Politics, Representation*, edited by Chitralekha Zutshi, pp. 265–83. New Delhi: Cambridge University Press.

Chowdhary, Rekha. 2014. '2009 Parliamentary Elections in Jammu and Kashmir'. In *Party Competition in Indian States: Electoral Politics in Post-Congress Polity*, edited by Suhas Palshikar, K.C. Suri, and Yogendra Yadav, pp. 190–209. New Delhi: Oxford University Press.

———. 2002. 'Lone's Liberal Legacy'. *Economic and Political Weekly*, 37 (25): 2398–400.

Das, Durga, ed. 1971. *Sardar Patel's Correspondence, 1945–50*. Vol. I: *New Light on Kashmir*. Ahmedabad: Navajivan Publishing House.

Datta, Ankur. 2016. *On Uncertain Ground: A Study of Displaced Kashmiri Pandits in Jammu and Kashmir*. New Delhi: Oxford University Press.

Duschinski, Haley, Mona Bhan, Ather Zia, and Cynthia Mahmood, eds. 2018. *Resisting Occupation in Kashmir*. Philadelphia: University of Pennsylvania Press.

Editorial. 2003. 'Hurriyat at Crossroads'. *Economic and Political Weekly*, 38 (29): 3020–1.

Faheem, Farrukh. 2018. 'Interrogating the Ordinary: Everyday Politics and the Struggle for *Azadi* in Kashmir'. In *Resisting Occupation in Kashmir*, edited by Haley Duschinski, Mona Bhan, Ather Zia, and Cynthia Mahmood, pp. 230–47. Philadelphia: University of Pennsylvania Press.

Gadru, S.N., ed. 1973. *Kashmir Papers: British Intervention in Kashmir, Including Arthur Brinckman's Wrongs of Cashmere, Robert Thorp's Kashmir Misgovernment, and Sir William Digby's Condemned Unheard.* Srinagar: Freethought Literature.

Gagnè, Karine. 2017. 'Building a Mountain Fortress for India: Sympathy, Imagination and the Reconfiguration of Ladakh into a Border Area'. *South Asia: Journal of South Asian Studies*, 40 (2): 222–38.

Ganguly, Sumit. 2016. *Deadly Impasse: Kashmir and Indo-Pakistani Relations at the Dawn of a New Century.* New York: Cambridge University Press.

———, ed. 2003. *The Kashmir Question: Retrospect and Prospect.* Oxon: Frank Cass and Company.

———. 1997. *The Crisis in Kashmir: Portents of War, Hopes of Peace.* New York: Cambridge University Press.

Ghai, Ved Kumari. 1968. *A Cultural and Literary Study of a Kashmiri Purana.* Srinagar: Jammu and Kashmir Academy of Art, Culture, and Languages.

Gupta, Radhika. 2014. 'Poetics and Politics of Borderland Dwelling: Baltis in Kargil'. *SAMAJ*, 10: 1–18.

Hamdani, Sameer. 2016. 'Restoration of the Thag Baba Shrine in Kashmir: A Forgotten Mughal Tomb for an Intoxicated Sufi Saint'. *International Journal of Islamic Architecture*, 5 (1): 165–202.

Hangloo, R.L. 2000. *The State in Medieval Kashmir.* Delhi: Manohar.

Hans, Asha. 2004. 'Women across Borders in Kashmir—the Continuum of Violence'. In *Peace Studies: An Introduction to the Concept, Scope, and Themes*, edited by Ranabir Samaddar, pp. 268–91. New Delhi: Sage.

Hassnain, Fida M. 2009. 'The Impact of Muslim Rule on the Kashmiri Society during the 14th and 15th Centuries'. *The Journal of Kashmir Studies*, 3 (1): 6–36.

Hussain, Shahla. undated. 'Kashmir's Cry for Freedom: Questions of Identity, Sovereignty, and Self-Determination'. Unpublished manuscript.

Inden, Ronald. 2008. 'Kashmir as Paradise on Earth'. In *The Valley of Kashmir: The Making and Unmaking of a Composite Culture?* edited by Aparna Rao, pp. 523–61. Delhi: Manohar.

———. 2000. 'Imperial Puranas: Kashmir as Vaissnava Center of the Words'. In *Querying the Medieval: Texts and the History of Practices in South Asia*, by Ronald Inden, Jonathan Walters, and Daud Ali, pp. 29–98. New York: Oxford University Press.

Junaid, Mohamad. 2018. 'Epitaphs as Counterhistories: Martyrdom, Commemoration, and the Work of Graveyards in Kashmir'. In *Resisting Occupation in Kashmir*, edited by Haley Duschinski, Mona Bhan, Ather Zia, and Cynthia Mahmood, pp. 248–77. Philadelphia: University of Pennsylvania Press.

Kabir, Ananya Jahanara. 2009. *Territory of Desire: Representing the Valley of Kashmir*. Minnesota: University of Minnesota Press.

Kak, Sanjay. 2013a. 'The Fire Is at My Heart: An Introduction'. In *Until My Freedom Has Come: The New*

Intifada in Kashmir, edited by Sanjay Kak, pp. ix–xxiv. Chicago: Haymarket Books.

———, ed. 2013b. *Until My Freedom Has Come: The New Intifada in Kashmir*. Chicago: Haymarket Books.

Kaul, Shonaleeka. 2018. *The Making of Early Kashmir: Landscape and Identity in the Rajatarangini*. New Delhi: Oxford University Press.

———. 2013. 'Kalhana's Kashmir: Aspects of the Literary Production of Space in the *Rajatarangini*'. *Indian Historical Review*, 40 (2): 207–22.

Kaul, Suvir. 2015. *Of Gardens and Graves: Essays on Kashmir. Poems in Translation*. Gurgaon: Three Essays Collective.

Kazi, Seema. 2018. 'Law, Gender and Governance in Kashmir'. In *Kashmir: History, Politics, Representation*, edited by Chitralekha Zutshi, pp. 150–71. New Delhi: Cambridge University Press.

———. 2010. *In Kashmir: Gender, Militarization & the Modern Nation-State*. Brooklyn, NY: South End Press.

Khan, Nyla Ali, ed., 2012. *The Parchment of Kashmir: History, Society, and Polity*. New York: Palgrave Macmillan.

Khan, Sardar Muhammad Ibrahim. 1965. *The Kashmir Saga*. Lahore: Ripon Printing Press.

Korbel, Josef. 1954. 'The National Conference Administration of Kashmir, 1949–1954'. *Middle East Journal*, 8 (3): 283–94.

Koul, Anand. 1991 [1924]. *The Kashmiri Pandit*. Delhi: Utpal Publication.

Kreutzmann, Hermann. 2015. 'Boundaries and Space in Gilgit-Baltistan'. *Contemporary South Asia* 23 (3): 276–91.

Leake, Elisabeth, and Daniel Haines. 2017. 'Lines of (In) Convenience: Sovereignty and Border-Making in South Asia, 1947–1965'. *The Journal of Asian Studies*, 76 (4): 963–85.

Mahmud, Ershad. 2018. 'The Contingencies of Everyday Life in Azad Jammu and Kashmir'. In *Resisting Occupation in Kashmir*, edited by Haley Duschinski, Mona Bhan, Ather Zia, and Cynthia Mahmood, pp. 211–29. Philadelphia: University of Pennsylvania Press.

Maskiell, Michelle. 2002. 'Consuming Kashmir: Shawls and Empires, 1500–2000'. *Journal of World History*, 13 (1): 27–65.

Mattoo, A.M. 1988. *Kashmir under the Mughals, 1586–1752*. Kashmir: Golden Horde Enterprises.

Michell, George. 2011. *Mughal Architecture and Gardens*. Suffolk: Antique Collectors' Club.

Noorani, A.G., ed. 2011. *Article 370: A Constitutional History of Jammu and Kashmir*. New Delhi: Oxford University Press.

Obrock, Luther. 2013. 'History at the End of History: Srivara's *Jainatarangini*'. *The Indian Economic and Social History Review*, 50 (2): 221–36.

Ogura, Satoshi. 2015. 'Linguistic Cosmopolitanism, Political Legitimacies, and Religious Identities in Sahmirid Kashmir (1339–1561)'. Paper presented at The Third Perso-Indica Conference, Delhi University, 3–4 September.

Parmu, R.K. 1969. *A History of Muslim Rule in Kashmir, 1320–1819.* Delhi: People's Publishing House.

Pollock, Sheldon. 2001. 'The Death of Sanskrit'. *Comparative Studies in Society and History*, 43 (2): 392–426.

Raghavan, Srinath. 2010. *War and Peace in Modern India.* New York: Palgrave Macmillan.

Rai, Mridu. 2018a. 'The Indian Constituent Assembly and the Making of Hindus and Muslims in Jammu and Kashmir'. *Asian Affairs*, 49 (2): 205–21.

———. 2018b. 'To "Tear the Mask off the Face of the Past": Archeology and Politics in Jammu and Kashmir'. In *Kashmir: History, Politics, Representation*, edited by Chitralekha Zutshi, pp. 25–50. New Delhi: Cambridge University Press.

———. 2004. *Hindu Rulers, Muslim Subjects: Islam, Rights, and the History of Kashmir.* New Delhi, Permanent Black.

Robinson, Cabieri DeBergh. 2013. *Body of Victim, Body of Warrior: Refugee Families and the Making of Kashmiri Jihadists.* Berkeley: University of California Press.

Rose, Leo E. 1992. 'The Politics of Azad Kashmir'. In *Perspectives on Kashmir: The Roots of Conflict in South Asia*, edited by Raju G.C. Thomas, pp. 235–53. Boulder, CO: Westview Press.

Roy Kumkum. 2010. *The Power of Gender & the Gender of Power: Explorations in Early Indian History.* New Delhi: Oxford University Press.

———. 2003. 'The Making of a Mandala: Fuzzy Frontiers of Kalhana's Kashmir'. In *Negotiating India's Past: Essays in Memory of Partha Sarathi Gupta*, edited by Biswamoy

Pati, Bhairabi Prasad Sahu, and T.K. Venkatasubramanian, pp. 52–66. New Delhi: Tulika Books.

Saraf, Muhammad Yusuf. 1979. *Kashmiris Fight—For Freedom*, vol. II, *1947–1978*. Lahore: Ferozsons.

———. 1977. *Kashmiris Fight—For Freedom*, vol. I, *1819–1946*. Lahore: Ferozsons.

Schild, Pascale. 2015. 'Local Politics of Reconstruction along and across Azad Kashmir's Border with Pakistan'. *Contemporary South Asia*, 23 (3): 292–313.

Sharma, Mahesh. 2008. 'Puranic Texts from Kashmir: Vitasta and River Ceremonials from the *Nilamata Purana*'. *South Asia Research*, 28 (2): 123–45.

Sikand, Yoginder. 2010. 'Jihad, Islam, and Kashmir: Syed Ali Shah Geelani's Political Project'. *Economic and Political Weekly*, 45 (40): 125–34.

Snedden, Christopher. 2018. 'Azad Kashmir: Integral to India, Integrated into Pakistan, Lacking Integrity as an Autonomous Entity'. In *Kashmir: History, Politics, Representation*, edited by Chitralekha Zutshi, pp. 113–31. New Delhi: Cambridge University Press.

———. 2015. *Understanding Kashmir and Kashmiris*. London: Hurst & Company.

———. 2012. *The Untold Story of the People of Azad Kashmir*. New York: Columbia University Press.

Sökefeld, Martin. 2018. '"Not Part of Kashmir, but of the Kashmir Dispute": The Political Predicaments of Gilgit-Baltistan'. In *Kashmir: History, Politics, Representation*, edited by Chitralekha Zutshi, pp. 132–49. New Delhi: Cambridge University Press.

————. 2015a. 'Introduction: Jammu and Kashmir—Boundaries and Movements'. *Contemporary South Asia*, 23 (3): 251–65.

————. 2015b. 'At the Margins of Pakistan: Political Relationships between Gilgit–Baltistan and Azad Jammu and Kashmir'. In *Pakistan's Political Labyrinths*, edited by Ravi Kalia, pp. 174–88. New York: Routledge.

————. 2005. 'From Colonialism to Postcolonial Colonialism: Changing Modes of Domination in the Northern Areas of Pakistan'. *The Journal of Asian Studies*, 64 (4): 939–74.

Sufi, G.M.D. 1974 [1949]. *Kashir: Being a History of Kashmir*, 2 vols. New Delhi: Light and Life Publishers.

Thomas, Raju G.C., ed. 1992. *Perspectives on Kashmir: Roots of Conflict in South Asia*. Boulder, CO: Westview Press.

Tikku, G.L. 1971. *Persian Poetry in Kashmir, 1339–1846: An Introduction*. Berkeley: University of California Press.

Tremblay, Reeta Chowdhari. 2018. 'Contested Governance, Competing Nationalisms and Disenchanted Publics: Kashmir beyond Intractability?' In *Kashmir: History, Politics, Representation*, edited by Chitralekha Zutshi, pp. 220–44. New Delhi: Cambridge University Press.

Tremblay, Reeta Chowdhari, and Mohita Bhatia. 2015. 'Kashmir's Contentious Politics: The More Things Change, the More They Stay the Same'. In *India's 2014 Elections: A Modi-Led BJP Sweep*, edited by Paul Wallace, pp. 231–57. New Delhi: Sage Publications.

Wani, Gull. 2014. 'Sub-Regional Conflicts and Selective Autonomy in J&K: Hill Councils in Power'. *Race & Class*, 56 (2): 81–92.

Whitehead, Andrew. 2015. 'The People's Militia: Communists and Kashmiri Nationalism in the 1940s'. In *Partition: The Long Shadow*, edited by Urvashi Butalia, pp. 128–54. New Delhi: Zubaan.

―――. 2007. *A Mission in Kashmir*. New Delhi: Penguin.

Zia, Ather. 2018. 'The Killable Kashmiri Body: The Life and Execution of Afzal Guru'. In *Resisting Occupation in Kashmir*, edited by Haley Duschinski, Mona Bhan, Ather Zia, and Cynthia Mahmood, pp. 103–28. Philadelphia: University of Pennsylvania Press.

Zutshi, Chitralekha. 2018a. 'Contesting Urban Space: Shrine Culture and the Discourse on Kashmiri Muslim Identities and Protest in the Late Nineteenth and Early Twentieth Centuries'. In *Kashmir: History: Politics, Representation*, edited by Chitralekha Zutshi, pp. 51–69. New Delhi: Cambridge University Press.

―――, ed. 2018b. *Kashmir: History, Politics, Representation*. New Delhi: Cambridge University Press.

―――. 2017. 'Seasons of Discontent and Revolt in Kashmir'. *Current History*, April: 123–9.

―――. 2015. 'An Ongoing Partition: History, Borders, and the Politics of Vivisection in Jammu and Kashmir'. *Contemporary South Asia*, 23 (3): 266–75.

―――. 2014. *Kashmir's Contested Pasts: Narratives, Sacred Geographies, and the Historical Imagination*. New Delhi: Oxford University Press.

―――. 2009. '"Designed for Eternity": Kashmiri Shawls, Empire, and Cultures of Production and Consumption in Mid-Victorian Britain'. *Journal of British Studies*, 48: 420–40.

———. 2004. *Languages of Belonging: Islam, Regional Identity, and the Making of Kashmir*. New York: Oxford University Press.

Index

About the Author

Chitralekha Zutshi is professor of history at The College of William & Mary, Virginia, USA. She specializes in nationalism, history writing, and political culture in South Asia. Her books include *Kashmir: History, Politics, Representation* (2018); *Kashmir's Contested Pasts: Narratives, Sacred Geographies, and the Historical Imagination* (2014); and *Languages of Belonging: Islam, Regional Identity, and the Making of Kashmir* (2004).